TIPTON'S CREW

Copyright © 1994 by Beautiful America Publishing Co.©
All rights reserved.
No portion of this book may be
reproduced in any form without written permission.

Library of Congress Catalog Card Number 94-37481
ISBN 0-89802-492-7

Published by **Beautiful America Publishing**©
P.O. Box 646, Wilsonville, Oregon 97070
503-682-0173

Authors: P. La Ferriere and Vernon L. Burda
Design: Heather Kier

Printed in U.S.A.

TIPTON'S CREW

P. La Ferriere & Vernon L. Burda

Beautiful America Publishing Company

Contents

Prologue—Tipton's Crew 1

Prologue Two—Tipton's Crew 5

Birth of a Crew 9

Preparation for Combat 17

Tragedy 31

Prisoners of War 45

Stalag Luft III 51

Exodus 63

PROLOGUE
TIPTON'S CREW

AUGUST 5, 1989—BUDAPEST, HUNGARY

Out of breath little Joshua Lassu rushed and stumbled as fast as his five year old legs would go, up the stairs from the basement of his home in Budapest, Hungary, down the hall and into the room where his father, Arpad, was just getting dressed. "Papa, Papa," little Joshua exclaimed. "Come see what I have found." Arpad could not help but notice the excitement in Joshua's eyes and feel some of the elation that his son expressed.

"What is it, Joshua, what is it? Just calm down and tell me what you have found."

"I don't know, I just don't know—but I know it is something" Joshua answered. "You remember that old, old suitcase which has been hiding in back of the dark corner? Well, today our cat, Max, knocked it over and the lock sprung open. You know how curious I am Papa, so I went over to the suitcase and I saw many, many pieces of metal with words stamped in them. Maybe they are secret treasure. I took one of them and I brought it for you."

Joshua then gave his father a small metal tag with letters and numbers stamped in it. Arpad could not read it, but he did know that it was in English, and he could make out one word, "TIPTON."

More curious than excited, Arpad said to little Joshua, "Come, let us go to the basement and we will find just what kind of treasure you have found." Whereupon Arpad and Joshua travelled back down the hall and down the steps into the dingy basement. The light was so poor that Arpad could not readily see just what was in the suitcase so he determined to take the suitcase to his study. He closed the suitcase and, lifting it carefully so he would not spill its curious contents, he carried it under one arm back to his study.

Arriving at his study he carefully opened the case and immediately saw about one hundred of those small, metal tags, all with English words engraved into the tags.

Arpad was perplexed. He tried to visualize how those tags should just now, after many, many years, come into little Joshua's hands. Arpad knew that before World War II and up to 1940 his father had lived in this house and sometime soon after that the dreaded German SS had taken over the house as the official residence of one of their Commandants. His father had told him that this Commandant was in charge of the Prison at Budapest during that war—and that the stories of the cruelty and killing at that prison during that time were repeated to that day.

Sending little Joshua out to play, Arpad sat at his desk in his study and examined the items more closely. It became clear to him that these were some type of identification tags. After further study he could plainly see that they were identification tags of American soldiers.

Arpad then began the task of sorting the tags by the names impressed onto each tag. When he had complete this task he found that there were 150 tags—mostly individual tags, but some were duplicates. All in all the tags represented 126 officers and enlisted men—one officer being Lt. Dale Tipton.

Arpad thought to himself "Here it is August of 1989—World War II has been over for 44 years—probably many of these men were no longer alive and probably most of the others have long ago forgotten all about these identification tags, or at the least had acquired new ones to replace them." Because of these thoughts Arpad determined to merely put the tags back into the small suitcase with the thought that he would turn them over to someone at the American Embassy in Budapest.

The next day Arpad took the small suitcase under his arm once more and took the tram through Budapest to the American Embassy. Upon ringing the bell at the Embassy he was approached by a Marine Guard who politely asked the purpose of his visit. Arpad showed the identification tags to the Marine Guard and pointed to the writing on the tag of Lt. Dale Tipton.

The Marine Guard immediately recognized them for what they were—identification tags from World War II, commonly called "Dog Tags." He quickly escorted Arpad to the office of Colonel Ruth Anderson who was the Defense and Air Attache to the American Embassy. Upon being introduced to Colonel Anderson, Arpad stated, "I have documentary evidence regarding 126 American service men." Being curious as to just what this "documentary evidence" was, Colonel Anderson had Arpad seat himself, and said "That is wonderful, now just what is this documentary evidence you have to show me?"

Arpad with a great show opened the small suitcase and spilled the 150 dog tags onto the desk of Colonel Anderson. Then quickly, before she had time to respond, he told her the tale of how his son Joshua found the tags, and the history of the occupancy of his house. Colonel Anderson thereupon thanked Arpad for his foresight in delivering the dog tags to the Embassy, and promised him that she would forward them to the proper authorities. Arpad left the Embassy with a warm feeling from the gratitude expressed to him for his actions.

The tags were in due course forwarded to the Army Personnel Command—which did catalog the tags and later informed Colonel Anderson that of the 126 men identified by the tags, 41 had died in Prisoner of War Camps throughout Germany, and the remainder were prisoners until liberated.

PROLOGUE TWO
TIPTON'S CREW

AUGUST 25, 1990—WALTHAM, MASSACHUSETTS

A large group of veterans and their wives were gathered in the main ballroom of the Boston Vista Waltham Hotel in anticipation of a gala evening of comradeship for a reunion of the members of the 781st Bomb Squadron based in Pantanella, Italy, during World War II. The July issue of the "Pantanella News" distributed by the 781st Bomb Squadron Association, in setting out the program for the forthcoming reunion had promised "some surprises during the evening program" and this only added to the suspense of the evening. After preliminary activities and program presentations, James Althoff, President of the Association, addressed the gathering and stated, "Tonight I have the honor and the privilege of presenting to you a representative of the United States Air Force who will make some presentations to some of you attending this gathering this evening. This matter was not on the original program when this meeting was planned, but recently the Air Force came into possession of some items belonging to six of our comrades. Two of those former comrade are deceased—Dale Tipton and Hulitt Holcomb-and one, Eugene Weiss, could not attend this meeting. However, three of those comrades are with us tonight, and I can tell you they do not know anything about this matter. These presentations to Harold Farrar, Frank Jasicko and Eugene Krzyzynski will come as a wonderful surprise to them. I now present to you Lt. General Gordon Fornell of the United States Air Force."

General Fornell arose slowly from his chair, looked over the audience for a full thirty seconds, then stated, "As a representative of the United States Air Force I am here tonight to make a presentation to three of you attending—the three being former members of Tipton's Crew. Dale Tipton, as most of you know, was the pilot of the B-24 bomber with the name 'Crescent of the Half Moon.' Most of you also know this airplane with its crew was shot down during a mission over Vienna in July of 1944. Tipton's crew became a famous crew to this squadron, for it was the only crew to be shot down twice by enemy fire—once by flak while on a mission over Ploesti, Romania, and the last time by enemy fighters. Tipton's entire crew evaded the enemy and eventually joined with Marshall Tito's Partisans fighting the Germans in Yugoslavia. After being rescued by the OSS and taken back to the base at Pantanella this crew could have returned to the United States. Instead, they chose to remain with their comrades and continue the fight.

"And they did continue the fight, flying many more missions, being exposed to enemy fighters and flak, with one member, Vernon Burda, being wounded in action, and another crew member performing a heroic feat which saved the aircraft and its grateful crew.

"However, their active participation in the fight ended on July 16, 1944, when enemy fighters attacked the formation in which they were flying, and the plane in which they had flown many, many missions, the good old 'Crescent of the Half Moon,' was hit and disabled.

"Through Dale Tipton's efforts the plane was kept in the air for some time—but the crew had to bail out near Zagreb, Yugoslavia, and all were captured by the enemy. Tipton's crew was taken to a prison near Budapest, Hungary, where they were stripped of their belongings and held for several days—some being beaten during this time.

"Tipton's crew was later split up and the officers were sent to the infamous Stalag Luft III. This was the camp made famous by the true to life movie, 'The Great Escape.' At the end of the war all of the crew members were liberated after being prisoners for about ten months and returned home.

"But tonight, after some 45 years have elapsed, I want to present to and return something to three of those men who are present at this banquet. Arrangements have been made to present these same items to the two deceased members of Tipton's crew and to Eugene Weiss, who could not be here tonight. So, if Eugene Krzyzynski, Harold Farrar, and Frank Jasicko will please come forward at this time."

Somewhat uncertain and thoroughly confused, the three men left the table where they had been sitting with former crew members Vernon Burda and Mike Deironimi and stood by General Fornell. General Fornell then again faced the group and told the audience the history of the missing dog tags, and ended by saying "The Army Personnel Command has given me the privilege of returning these dog tags to their rightful owners at this time—so I present to you, and to each of you, your dog tags which were taken from you in July of 1944—and thank you for what you have done."

The emotion of that moment was too great for all three men and tears came to their eyes as they so clearly recalled those moments at Budapest. For a moment they could not speak, their throats were so choked up. The whole crowd respected their feelings, and a total silence descended upon the banquet hall. After some time Eugene Krzyzynski finally was able to utter in a choked voice, "Thank you, we all thank you," and the three returned slowly to their seats where their wives and loved ones comforted them.

Then General Fornell in his final statement said, "If only the dog tags and those dog tags of the rest of Tipton's crew could speak—what a wonderful story they would tell."

BIRTH OF A CREW

NOVEMBER, 1943—DAVIS MONTHAN AIR BASE—TUCSON, ARIZONA

This airfield was a beehive of activity. A brand new group with several squadrons was being formed. Planes were being gathered and crews assembled. Pilots, co-pilots, navigators, bombardiers, gunners, radio operators, crew-chiefs and crew members were being assembled from bases all over the United States where they had received extensive training just for this purpose.

The railroad depot in Tucson displayed its usual frantic wartime activity. Trains were arriving, trains were leaving, troops were embarking, troops were disembarking, soldiers, sailors, air men, all seemed to be in a state of mass confusion. Yet somehow some semblance of order seemed to rise above the seemingly disorganized crowds.

Arriving on track #4 was a train from Salt Lake City, and almost at the instant that it came to a halt a stream of servicemen poured from the train. One, 2nd Lieutenant Gene Krzyzynski, stepped from the train with his luggage in his hand, and, after looking around, walked to a bus marked "Davis Monthan Field." Upon entering the vehicle he proceeded to an empty seat near the center of the bus and gazed at the amazing sight of this western town with its Mexican flavor. It seemed to him that he had been transported to a different country far different from his home in Buffalo, New York.

In the packet which he carried in his hand were his orders which on the face seemed quite simple—he was to report to Davis Monthan Air Base where he would be assigned to a crew of a new squadron of a new group just being formed—the 781st Squadron of the 465th Bomb Group. Gene was really excited. It really meant a lot to him to be able to start from scratch with a brand new crew, with a brand new airplane in a brand new squadron which would start its final training as one body of airmen. They would become as closely knit with each other as was possible during this extensive and concentrated training period.

Krzyzynski disembarked from the bus after it had entered the field and immediately reported to Headquarters. There he was assigned to bachelor officers quarters in barrack B-2 and notified that he had been assigned as bombardier in the crew of 1st Lieutenant Dale Tipton—who would also be his roommate in barrack B-2.

Krzyzynski realized at once that this was a historic moment in his life. Here he was, finally starting on a period which would be the most exciting, the most dangerous, and the most fulfilling of his life. He could hardly wait to get started as he rapidly strode toward barrack B-2. Arriving there he checked the assignment ledger and found that he was to be in room 27 on the second floor. Lt. Tipton had already checked in.

Krzyzynski hastened up the steps to the second floor and after knocking once entered room 27. The room was sparsely furnished—but adequate. At least the beds looked comfortable. One bed was apparently taken by Lt. Tipton as it was almost entirely covered with his gear. Krzyzynski placed his B-4 clothes bag on the other bed and then made his discovery tour of the 2nd floor—especially to find the shower room and the latrine. Upon his return to his room he was pleasantly surprised to see one of the biggest men he had ever seen. Approaching him, he extended his hand and said, "I hope that you are Lt. Tipton."

"Well," Tipton said, "let me check my dog tags and we will see about that. What do you know, you are absolutely right, I am Dale Tipton—but don't call me 'Dale,' just call me 'Tip'."

"I'm surely glad to meet you, Tip, since I am not only going to be your roommate, but I see that I am going to be the bombardier on your crew." Gene replied. "I am Eugene Krzyzynski but for gosh sakes just call me 'Chris'—it's hard enough for Polish people to pronounce Krzyzynski let alone anyone else to get two zy's in there. It shortens up all conversations if people just call me 'Chris'."

Tipton laughed at that and in turn said "Well, Chris, since we are really going to be close physically and mighty close mentally, for the next few months and maybe years, tell me all about yourself. I take it that you are about twenty years old—are a well built Polish bombardier, and could be a woman killer with your handsome face. Outside of that you might start from the beginning and tell me more."

"Well, to begin with, you are right. I am Polish and I am twenty years old—though I don't know about that handsome face and to this date I really haven't seemed to impress many woman. I really have been pretty busy since my junior year in high school when we all heard about Pearl Harbor.

"To begin with, of course, I was born—and you are right, I am twenty years old being born on February 4, 1923, in Buffalo, New York. Unfortunately my father died about one year later, and I am really sorry that I did not have that close contact with a father as most kids did. I am sure that my mother tried to make up for this by giving me all the love and affection she could. But then my mother died when I was in the 7th grade of St. John Kanty parochial school. Thereafter my four sisters and one brother took over the chore, with the help of the Nuns at school, of raising this Polish child. I can tell you, Tip, that there was never a shortage of love and guidance given to me. Unfortunately it took me many years to realize how fortunate I was to have had their love and their care.

"From an early date I was always interested in flying and in aviation and in airplanes. Charles Lindbergh was one of my early heroes—especially since our birth dates were on the same day. At any rate, I pursued a course of aviation mechanics at Burgard Vocational High School in Buffalo. Right after Pearl Harbor I wanted to enlist, but my sisters and brother talked me out of it. They did recommend that I work nights for an aircraft company in Buffalo until I graduated.

"I did that, but as soon as I graduated I told them that I could not stand it any longer and that I was going to enlist in the service. I first tried to enlist in the Navy, but when I went to enlist I saw that the line was well over a block long, so I turned around and went to the U.S. Army recruiting station. The recruiter told me that since I was a high school graduate and had taken Aviation Mechanics in high school and had worked for an aircraft company that I really should take the exam and apply for an appointment as an Aviation Cadet. So I did. I passed the exam and enlisted in the service on October 20, l942—just about one year ago."

"My God," said Tipton "Just to think that in one year a young nineteen year old American could be taken from high school, trained in basic training, take further training, and become an officer. Soon he would have to be ready to go to Europe or somewhere as a crew member of a big four engine bomber with nine other crew members. They would not be much older than he, and probably with just as limited a time in the service—to fight, and maybe die, for their country! I know that physically we all can do it, but I wonder if we have the experience and mental balance to handle all of the problems that I see coming up. I really have actually prayed to God that we will have the best crew in this whole squadron—a crew whose members care for each other, a crew that is so competent that crew members will not have any qualms about flying in this crew. A crew whose members do not drink nor carouse around, a crew whose members have the attitude that they can perform the way we are going to be trained to perform—in other words, one damn good team."

"I know this, Tip," Chris replied, "you can count on me to the best of my ability—and I do share your wishes and desires. You know I really started my Cadet training to become a pilot—had about twenty-two of the required 40 hours of pilot training in the Fairchild PT-19 when I sprained my ankle and got so far behind my class that I washed out. I had a choice then of becoming a navigator or a bombardier—and I chose to become a bombardier. I really think I am a good one, Tip, and I hope I can prove it to you and to our whole crew. I will pledge to you that I will try to be the best crew member of Tipton's crew."

Little did either man know that in less than six months Lt. Krzyzynski would perform an act of heroism which would save the lives of the entire crew while flying on a bombing mission over enemy territory.

Tipton was moved by his sincerity and grasped his hand and said, "If the rest of the crew has that same desire and guts, I can tell you now, Chris, we are going to have the kind of crew that we both want. As for me, there is not much to tell. I grew up in Los Angeles, and since I really was a good football player, I attended the University of Southern California where I turned out to be a pretty good tackle—in fact some thought I was a very good tackle. But when the war came along things changed. You must realize that being on the West Coast we really were affected by the attack on Pearl Harbor, and it did drive home to all of us the importance of doing our part.

"I joined the Army Air Force as a Cadet and received my wings and the gold bars of a 2nd Lieutenant. I really wanted to be a fighter pilot as I love action when I am in the air—but you must realize, Chris, that with my size and weight—about 250 pounds—they would have had to build bigger fighters to accommodate me. So, of course, I ended up becoming a bomber pilot. I became an instructor for other pilots, and I can tell you I think I will be a lot better off flying in combat than flying with those students every day—my chances of survival will be 100 percent better."

"How about the rest of our crew, Tip?" Chris then asked. "Do you have a list of all of them, and do you know something about some of them."

"You talk about an All American Crew," Tip replied, "We've really got it. We've got two Czechs, one Pole, a Greek, an Italian, and a German. As I understand it, all of them can speak in their foreign tongue. I tell you, if we ever get shot down over enemy territory in Europe and escape or evade the enemy we should be able to get along no matter where we are."

When he made that statement Tip did not realize that in less than seven months the entire crew would be shot down over enemy territory and would escape by joining up with partisans. The ability of the members of the crew to speak those languages proved to be invaluable.

Looking at his roster, Tip then read the names of the ten men who would train from the very beginning as a crew, who would fly over thirty missions together, who would be shot down not only once, but twice, together, who would all know the effects of being prisoners of war for over ten months, and who would, during the rest of their lives, appreciate the comradeship and abilities of the individual members of this crew—Tipton's Crew.

Tipton then handed the list of names of the rest of the crew to Chris who read off—"Eugene Weiss, Vernon Burda, Albert Ralston, William Soteropoulos, Michael Deironimi, Frank Jasicko, Harold Farrar, and Hulitt Holcomb."

"I see what you mean when you said we have an all American crew, Tip. We're so darn lucky that we can train as a crew from the beginning. As I understand it, we will get our own B-24 bomber here in the States and will fly overseas together in that plane and will fly most of our missions in that plane. I only hope we get through this together so we can fly it back to the states and still all be alive and well when this is all over, and still be one whole crew."

As it turned out the crew did get their plane and did fly over 30 combat missions together—but their plane, "The Crescent of the Half Moon," was shot down on their last combat flight and they did not get to fly it back to United States. Although this crew was shot down twice, evaded and escaped once, and spent over nine months as Prisoners of War—they did all get back to their loved ones. They still vividly remember many of the experiences they had as crew members. They still share a feeling towards each other that cannot be duplicated by others who have not shared the close relationships built up from their first meetings, and their complete reliance upon each other.

Neither Tip nor Chris had met the other officers of their new crew, their navigator Vernon Burda and their co-pilot Eugene Weiss. Tipton had met a navigator, Donald Barrett, who had been through navigation school with Burda. He had told Tipton that Burda had grown up in Dickinson, a small town in western North Dakota. After graduation from high school there and attending Drake University for two years, Burda volunteered for Glider Pilot Training and did complete that training, getting his Glider Pilot Wings and a S/Sgt rating. When the Air Corps cut back that program because they simply had too many glider pilots, Burda was offered an opportunity to enter cadet training as a future navigator. It was there that he met Don Barrett who became one of his best friends and this friendship continued for more than 50 years.

Tipton had asked Barrett to describe Burda and Barrett had replied, "That guy proceeds through life at about 125% the normal pace and never hides himself behind affectations—what you see is what you get. Also, be careful because he disarms you with his toothy grin and direct approach. You only become aware of his intelligence slowly. Another thing, Burda is extremely loyal to his friends and you can bet he will be a real asset to your crew."

Tipton and Chris then went to the officers' club where there was a constant roar of mixed sounds as crew members of the newly formed 781st Bomb Squadron were all finally meeting their fellow Officers. Tipton noticed that Colonel McKenna was sitting by himself at one of the small tables so he walked across the room and joined him.

"Have you had any word on my co-pilot yet?" Tipton asked. "Not really, Tip." replied Colonel McKenna, "In fact, I don't think you will have a co-pilot assigned until you get to McCook Air Base at McCook, Nebraska. You know we all will be going up there within a month so many of the crews will not be completely filled until we get there."

"What will we be doing at McCook?" Tipton asked. "I can tell you this," replied the Colonel, "this squadron is going to be flying day and night on the most concentrated training schedule you can imagine. We will have to weld this squadron together as an efficient fighting unit in about two months time and be prepared to fly overseas and into combat within about three months. So you can see that we are really putting a big load on the shoulders of every pilot of every crew to get his crew in shape for combat in that time span."

"My God," Tipton replied," you really are putting something on our backs. Can you tell me this, since we probably will be going overseas from McCook, will we be able to have our wives join us at McCook for those two or three months?"

"As far as I can tell the wives can go to McCook, but you must realize that the living conditions will not be the best. The wives cannot stay on the base. McCook, Nebraska, is a very small town and even though the townspeople will probably throw their homes open to help the wives, the accommodations probably will not be great, and they surely will be crowded. There is one small hotel that I know of and that is about all. And of course, you must realize that with our busy flying schedule you will not be able to spend much time with your wife."

"I know that," Tipton replied, "but if this is our last time to be together, whatever time we have we must share—and I know that my wife feels the same way. I will have her contact that small hotel immediately to see if she can at least get a room, even if she has to share it with one or two or more other wives."

PREPARATION FOR COMBAT

DECEMBER 10, 1943—ABOARD CROWDED TRAIN APPROACHING McCOOK, NEBRASKA

Jean Tipton and Jean Kennedy were sharing space on a railroad car which was crowded, dirty, and filled with cigarette smoke. They both were anxious to get to McCook to rejoin their husbands as they both knew in their hearts this was the last time that they would be together for some time. Immediately after this training period in McCook the whole squadron would be going overseas and engaging in combat with the enemy.

Jean Tipton turned to Jean Kennedy and said, "I just received a letter from Tip and if you like I will share it with you." Not waiting for an answer, Jean opened the envelope, took out a letter, and started to read.

December 7, 1943

Dear Jean,

Just think that it has been exactly two years to the day that we were attacked at Pearl Harbor—two years, and it feels like an eternity. I can hardly remember my life before the war and my life without you. We've only been apart such a short time, but I miss you so much that it hurts.

I finally have the rest of the crew together and we are training as a full crew. I think I am lucky to have the crew I have for they are really good in their jobs and I have never seen a more conscientious group. They don't smoke nor drink, except for a beer now and then, and seem to realize that we have only a short, short time to get fully prepared for whatever comes next.

This is a typical midwestern town of about 6000 people who are all extremely friendly and seem to want to give 100 percent of their energy to the war effort. You cannot realize how cold it is here. It must get down to zero every night. The first thing you had better do is to get some winter clothes. It is lot different from Tucson. However, it is clear and crisp which makes for good flying weather.

Every one in the crew is different, and I know that you will like them all. That Mike Deironimi is really a character right out of Damon Runyon's books about New York people. We cannot help but love him. He is always joking and if we ever want to get some unusual item—Mike will find it for us. We don't ask him how he got it, or where. He is the lower ball gunner and is small enough so that he doesn't have any trouble getting in and out of the ball turret.

Frank Jasicko is our crew chief, and he seems to be recognized as one of the very best. He is a Czech, as is Lt. Burda, and they really get along fine. The radio operator, Hulitt Holcomb, who doubles as a gunner, is from Oklahoma. We kid him a lot about his queer speaking. His wife is here and I know you will get to love her. Bill Soteropoulos is our nose gunner. As you can tell, he is Greek and he speaks the language so well that when things go wrong he can really cuss in Greek. Of course, we don't know what the heck he is saying.

Harold Farrar is our tail gunner. Right after high school he went to San Diego to work for Consolidated Aircraft to help in the war effort. After entering the army he was assigned to the Army Air Force and took his aerial gunnery at a school at Las Vegas. He is quiet and serious and competent—what more can we ask?

I don't know why, but they seem to want us to not associate with the enlisted men of our crew. I think that is crazy. Some of these officers think that because they have a gold or silver bar on their shoulders, they are above the enlisted men. The way I feel about it is that they all are just as good or better than we are. Not only that, we are going to depend upon each other for our very lives. I can tell you this, Jean, we are going to violate that rule and associate as if we are a family.

I can hardly wait until you get here. You must know that we will not have the time together that we both would like.

I love you.

Dale

Jean Tipton brushed a tear from her eye, just as the conductor loudly called "McCook, McCook—next stop in five minutes." Then the car broke into bedlam as everyone started gathering their possessions. Nobody had checked much luggage. There were boxes, bags, luggage, duffel bags, coats, hats, gloves and an assortment of loose material to gather in some sort of arrangement so that it could be removed in the shortest time.

Jean Tipton stepped from the train and saw a small depot facing one street in the town—which seemed to be the only street. It certainly was the main street. Luckily, the one small hotel was so close that she could easily walk to it. This was no easy task as she was burdened with so many items. Luckily, Tip had been able to get her the last available room in the hotel. Most of the wives had to stay with families in McCook who, thank God, went out of their way to provide some kind of accommodations.

Jean was shown to her small room and, after looking it over, sat on the bed and held her head. It was about 12' by 12' and had only a bed, toilet facilities, a small stand, small closet and one lamp. Jean, nevertheless was happy for she knew that it could be worse and the main thing was that she would be with Tip until he shipped out for overseas duty.

It was extremely cold and there was little heat in the room so everyone using the room had to have sweaters and jackets on. In fact, it was so cold in McCook that Jean would put food in the window where it would freeze and thus keep until used. Jean did find a small hot plate in a local hardware store and this was the extent of the cooking facilities of Tipton Manor, as this room was called. Jean had no cooking counter, so she obtained a small piece of lumber and placed it over the toilet. When the toilet was not in use, this was her cooking counter.

The crews were so busy now that they very seldom got into the town more than 6 or 7 hours at a time. Before dawn they would report for duty and start a most concentrated period to shake out all of the possible bugs. The crew would fly from 6 to 10 hours each day, and in between, try to take all the bugs out of their B-24. Jasicko, the crew chief, was especially busy tuning up this huge plane so that the crew could depend on it for their lives.

One episode almost grounded Tipton and Krzyzynski. One particular flight where they were to drop bombs at approximately 10 minute intervals, Tipton and Krzyzynski decided to drop two bombs instead of one and thus speed up the exercise. This was all right, except their flight log then had to be edited to show the proper intervals with reports of hits, etc.

They did not know that that very day one crew had unfortunately let a bomb go prematurely and had thus bombed the lumber yard in McCook. One can easily imagine the uproar that this caused throughout the whole squadron. When the flight logs of all of the crews were examined, the log of Tipton's crew was brought to light and Tipton and Krzyzynski were brought up for possible punishment. Naturally, they tried to prove their innocence and were partially successful. They were allowed to continue with their training. From then on, for 50 years, the story of the Tipton crew bombing the McCook lumber yard was told and retold by squadron members.

It was not until about 50 years later that Jim Althoff, editor of the "Pantanella News," published by the 781st Bomb Squadron Association in his July, 1991, edition, stated the following: *An Earlier report made the Tipton crew responsible for this famous raid on the McCook lumber yard. Information has now come forward that the Tipton Crew was not the crew that was responsible. My apologies to the Tipton Crew for this incorrect report. It was the Prince crew. The bombardier was Murray Septoff.*

Unfortunately, Tipton was not alive in 1991 to hear the good news. Jean Tipton and the remaining six members of the crew were only too happy to have that stigma removed from the name of Tipton's Crew.

On December 22, 1943, Tipton's Crew was flying formation at about 24,000 feet. Tipton was such a strong man and such a good pilot that the Crew swore that they could walk from their wing right into the open window of the plane next to them. Half way through the mission Deironimi noticed that Farrar looked as if he were sleeping, so he went back to kid him about it. To his surprise he noticed that Farrar's oxygen mask had come off and he was turning blue. At 24,000 feet there is not enough oxygen in the atmosphere to sustain human life. In fact, oxygen masks were ordered to be put on at the 10,000 feet level.

Deironimi quickly placed the oxygen mask over the face of Farrar and breathed a sigh of relief when he saw that Farrar's color gradually returned and he regained consciousness. Farrar was pale and totally exhausted for the rest of the flight. To this day he continues to thank Mike Deironimi for saving his life. It was estimated that if he had gone without oxygen for another 10 minutes he would not have survived.

Tipton's crew, contrary to the unofficial rules, fraternized and became a close knit family. Jean Tipton did complain to them constantly, and tried to stop their habit of entering Tipton's room, at any time, without knocking—but she really never did stop the habit. When Christmas came in 1943 the whole Crew somehow fit into the room together with Hulitt Holcomb's wife, Alice, and all had a Christmas dinner and sort of a farewell party. Farrar still was recovering from his brush with death and left early—but the rest had several hours of comradeship and good cheer. The whole crew and the wives knew that the time was drawing near for departure.

Almost immediately after that, Burda and his good friend, Don Barrett, and most of the navigators were flown to Geiger Field near Spokane, Washington, to take a concentrated course in celestial navigation. It had become common knowledge that they would have to navigate each of their planes individually all the way across the Atlantic Ocean from Brazil to Dakar in Africa. On this long flight the only method of navigation available to them would be celestial navigation, as a complete radio silence would to be required. Of course, there would be no landmarks. In fact the flight would be taken at night and would take over 12 hours.

Don Barrett and Burda really had a ball in Spokane. They had their dashing officer's uniforms and were young men in the prime of life. At the Davenport Hotel in Spokane there seemed to be quite a few young ladies who liked what they saw. Don Barrett and Burda met two nice young ladies and they limited their hours off of the base to seeing just those two. They felt a little sorry for the rest of Tipton's crew in freezing McCook, in cramped quarters, and working 14 to 16 hours a day while they only had to put in about 4 hours a day at school. The rest of the time they could enjoy the advantages of Spokane. However, they did not dwell too much on the problems of the rest of their crew. Don Barrett and Vern Burda became extremely close at that time and that relationship survived the war and for more than 50 years thereafter.

Finally the entire crew reassembled at McCook and finished the final month of hectic and accelerated training. In the opinion of the command staff the entire squadron was now ready for combat. It was determined that the plane commanders would fly their planes through Trinidad to Brazil, to Dakar, and to a base at Oudna, near Tunis, in the desert of Tunisia, while their permanent base at Pantanella, Italy, was being completed.

The ground crews would be transported by ship as well as most of the administrative staff. Eugene Weiss was extremely disappointed when Henry Willett was designated to fly as Tipton's co-pilot on the cross ocean trip, but he knew that he would be reunited later with the rest of Tipton's crew.

FEBRUARY 3, 1944

The entire air echelon flew to Lincoln, Nebraska. Tipton's crew arrived in Lincoln only hours before one of the largest blizzards to ever hit that town arrived. The snow, cold, and high wind forced them to stay there until February 12. Originally they were to stop only long enough to get their planes through their final checks and have installed any required guns, ammunition, etc. which might have been missing, and to get a final tune up.

Tipton's crew did not mind too much as Jean Tipton again followed Tip and stayed at the Cornhusker Hotel in Lincoln , which seemed like heaven. Handsome Eugene Krzyzynski seemed to be adored by all of the young women in the lounge at the Cornhusker hotel, but the rest of the crew usually just talked about their present plans and became much better acquainted with Henry Willett. The more they saw of Henry, the more they liked him.

FEBRUARY 12, 1944

The cold, the wind, and the snow finally cleared and the squadron flew to Morrison Field at West Palm Beach, Florida. Upon arrival Deironimi jumped from the plane and kissed the ground, and he took off his shirt and stripped himself of his long underwear. This was Florida! It seemed like heaven to all who had just left the cold and wind of Nebraska in February—it was warm, warm, warm!

Here Tipton's crew was not allowed off of the base, but merely spent the time getting ready for the final legs of their flight to Tunisia. They did all bask in the sun and really enjoyed the Florida weather and seemed to relax somewhat.

FEBRUARY 15, 1944

On a clear day most of the crews of the 781st Squadron took off individually on the first leg of the cross ocean flight. After take off they would be separated completely from other planes as strict radio silence had to be maintained at all times. Tipton's crew followed the Prince Crew by about 20 minutes with the first planned stop to be at Waller Field in Trinidad. Soon after take off Jasicko noticed that the right engine was not sounding right. After checking he determined that somehow it was losing oil. He reported this to Tipton, who, after consulting with Burda to see just where they were, decided to land at Berenquin Field in Puerto Rico. He feathered the propeller and approached Berenquin field on three good engines. With Willett's help he landed "Crescent of the Half Moon" with little trouble and reported the problem to the operations officer. The plane was then left in the capable hands of the ground crews and Tipton's crew was put up at the base.

The next day the operations officer informed Tipton that the problem had been solved, so the crew again boarded the plane and prepared for take off. However, after speeding down the runway and lifting off, both Tipton and Willett realized that the plane was sluggish and not responding to the controls. It was only the strength of Tipton, and ability of Willett, that the plane was held in the air. However, it did not gain enough elevation and the plane sheared off the top of a palm tree. Tipton again brought the plane back with a perfect landing and again reported to the operations officer who swore that this time the plane would get a complete 100% check-up.

During the three day layover the crew enjoyed the warmth and comforts of Berenquin Field. It seemed almost like a resort. It had nice beaches, wonderful Enlisted Men's Club and Officer Club. It even had a beautiful 18 hole golf course. So, of course, Tipton's crew did not suffer too much at this forced layover. Also, someone (without mentioning names) made contact with a supplier of rum and whiskey. Although it was against the rules, somehow several cases of these liquid refreshments were stashed aboard the plane before the final take off.

It might be said that the facilities at Berenquin Field were in stark contrast with the next planned permanent field at Oudna, North Africa. There the sand was not just in sand traps, but all over, and 30 feet deep. Their accommodations would be unheated tents and the food would be dished out with flies and sand as condiments.

After a successful take off at Berenquin Field the crew headed toward their next destination—Belem at the mouth of the Amazon River in Brazil. While flying over the thick jungles of Brazil Deironimi turned to Holcomb and said, "My God, just look at those trees. It is as if we are flying over an ocean made up of trees for as far as we can see, and we have been flying over them for over one hour."

"Yes," Holcomb answered, "and just remember this, we are to have complete radio silence, no matter what happens. You can see that as thick as that jungle is, our mothers and fathers would never see us again."

With this sobering thought, the crew watched the jungle go below them for hours, but finally approached Belem. At that point the Amazon River really looked like another Ocean—it was so wide. The only difference was that it was so muddy that it looked like a chocolate ocean. Just as the plane landed the crew was treated to one of those immense thunder showers that the area was famous for. The rain came down so fast and steady that one could not see over 20 feet. They all gave thanks that they had actually landed before it started. As quickly as it started it also stopped and the plane was parked for the night.

The next day the crew flew the plane for the shorter flight to Forteleza, Brazil. They all understood that this would be their final look at the North and South American continents. Because the next hop would be at night, over water all the way, and over 12 hours long. The final inspection by Jasicko, Tipton, and Willett was extremely fine-tuned. Burda, the navigator upon whose shoulders would rest the responsibility of getting them to the right spot at the right time, studied his charts one final time and made sure that his sextant was in good working order and that his watch was set on Greenwich Time so that his celestial navigation could be computed correctly and speedily. He planned to take a "fix" on the stars at least every half hour.

To take a "fix" to determine just where you were with celestial navigation one had to shoot at least two heavenly bodies, and preferably three, then draw your lines on a chart. see where the lines crossed, and there is where you should be. However, since you are flying all the time you are "shooting" the stars, moon, or planets, one must remember to advance the first and second lines to make up for this difference in time.

Somehow Burda achieved his goal and did get a fix every half hour. After the first three hours Tipton told him that he did not have to report further to him unless he saw that the plane was getting off course and needed corrections. The plane, meanwhile, was flying on automatic pilot. In this manner either Tipton or Willett could be getting some sleep. It was apparent to Burda that the rest of the crew were already asleep.

Soon after sunrise the coast of Africa came closer. Burda realized that this was the most important phase of his navigation for he had to know just where the plane was crossing onto the continent and he had to instruct Tipton which direction to turn to fly into Dakar. The plane was now almost out of fuel and if the plane were directed to fly away from Dakar, instead of toward Dakar, it would very soon be out of fuel and be forced down, still without radio communications. This, in fact, happened to at least two crews which never did show up at Dakar. A navigator on one of those planes, Blake, had been through navigation school with Burda and Barrett and this was their first loss of a friend.

Burda, upon approaching the coastline confidently told Tipton "Turn left when you pass the coast and you will see Dakar in about one half an hour." Then he crossed his fingers. Sure enough—in one half hour there it was—Dakar! Tipton landed the plane with no trouble and the entire crew was extremely relieved. They all told Burda what a great navigator he was. From then on they could only have complete faith in him. Burda kept to himself the fears that he had felt during that long trip.

After a short stop in Dakar for refueling the crew they took off for Marrakech in Morocco. Before coming to the Atlas Mountains and somewhere in the middle of the Sahara desert, Tipton saw a massive sand storm ahead—the father of all storms, he later stated. He could see the dust cloud clearly, black, and over 15,000 feet high. Quickly he asked Burda for directions to the nearest airfield of any kind. Burda informed him that, luckily, there was a small airfield at a French Foreign Legion oasis called Tindouf and gave Tipton the directions. Tipton immediately flew there and landed as quickly as he could.

The crew spent two days there and were quite taken by the difference in the culture which they found there. Deironimi delighted in taking pictures of the crew with camels and small mules and any other creatures. Soteropoulos, the Greek, dressed as an Arab and he actually could have passed as one.

The weather finally cleared and the crew took off for the next stop at Marrakech. It was clear all the way and Tipton landed with no trouble. Marrakech was famous as a resort for wealthy French families and the accommodations were more than adequate. A short time was spent here and some of the members of the crew ventured into the Casbah (Arab quarters) just to see if the movie versions of these places were accurate. They did not find any bars quite like the one in the movie "Casablanca" but they had a good taste of Arab culture in that walled section of town.

The final stop of this trip would be the next destination—Oudna in Tunisia. The crew really was anxious to get to this semi-permanent base, for at least they could call it home for a little while. Upon approaching the landing strip, Tipton saw that the runway was merely steel grates laid over the sand, and sand was everywhere. He landed successfully and the crew members crawled out of the plane and looked around. They did not see much. This still looked like it was in the middle of the desert.

Jasicko stayed with the plane while the rest of Tipton's crew checked in at operations and were assigned living quarters—which were not much. All four officers slept in a tent with an assortment of scorpions, flies and flying insects. The constant wind blew sand into the tents at all times and the nights would turn really cold, considering that this was Africa. Tipton and Willett built a jerry-rigged stove of sorts. It was half of an oil barrel turned upside down with a metal smoke stack going through the hole in the roof of the tent. Deironimi would somehow keep the tents supplied with high octane airplane fuel to be used as fuel for these stoves. Needless to say, there were quite a few accidents and explosions would occur quite often. Also, the smoke stacks would fill with soot at a rapid rate and Willett, being the lightest officer, would have to rope himself up the tent to the very top, where he would drop a rock tied to a rope down the stack to clear it free of soot.

Flying took on a desperate look as everyone knew that this was about the last practice which the squadron would have before combat. For some reason there was an unusual amount of emphasis on low level flying—a most dangerous thing to do. Actually, two planes and crews were lost when they had a mid-air collision during one of these practice runs. This loss put a real damper on the base for a couple of days. The first raid on the oil fields and refineries at Ploesti, Rumania, would be flown while the squadron was in North Africa. This would be an extremely long range raid, from North Africa all the way to Ploesti. The planes had to fly at extremely low altitudes so that the Germans could not locate them easily on their radar.

Since oil was what the German war machines ran on, the oil fields and refineries at Ploesti were extremely well defended, especially by flack. The German gunners at Ploesti were reputed to be the most accurate and the best gunners in the whole German army. The crews of the 781st, and Tipton's crew in particular, were to soon find this out as they made flight after flight from

Italy to Ploesti and suffered huge losses from that extremely accurate flack.

The desert Arabs, unlike those in Marrakech, were of a different sort. They would steal the gold from your teeth if they could. They were always wandering through the area and it was impossible to keep them out without a huge M.P. group available, but there was none. Many Arabs were traders and would trade for anything—clothing, food, cigarettes, guns, or anything they could haul. Tipton's crew soon found that the liquor that they had obtained in Puerto Rico was a very valuable commodity. They could get $35 a bottle for it or trade it for almost anything. Also, since none of the crew smoked they had cartons of cigarettes with which to barter. Mike Deironimi was the unofficial trader for Tipton's crew and he soon furnished them with chocolates, blankets, new shoes, sweaters and an assortment of items, which for all practical purposes, were useless in this God forsaken part of the earth. They later had a use in Italy.

The food was terrible. After standing in long lines to get it, it would be thrown on ones mess kit in one big blob. Every meal tasted the same. Every meal had its one common ingredient—sand. The lemons and oranges and other fruit that Deironimi obtained really helped the morale of Tipton's crew.

Outside of flying, there was nothing to do at this base as the facilities of a permanent base were non-existent. It was reputed that there was a tent of ill repute behind some sand dunes about a quarter of a mile from the living area and, from reports received, there were long lines of men waiting for the services they could receive there.

Tipton had a meeting with his crew soon after arriving at this base and told them that none of them were to drink excessively nor use the facilities of that Arab tent area. The crew respected him and respected each other, and it can be truthfully said that these instructions were obeyed to the letter.

One weekend the officers were allowed to go to Tunis. Burda and his good navigator friend Barrett took advantage of this and wandered through several blocks of the town. They had been warned not to drink any liquids offered to them, and they carried their own canteens. They did enjoy the trip, however, as it showed them a part of the world which they may have read about, but could not really understand until one actually saw at close range the people and the culture of that area—good and bad.

APRIL 27, 1944

Finally the air base at Pantanella, Italy, was completed enough, and the ground crews who had came across by ship had arrived. The other personnel, including Lt. Eugene Weiss, Tipton's co-pilot, had also arrived so the squadron was able to feel as if they had a home. Pantanella is in the Eastern part of Italy, almost directly across from Naples and quite close to Bari. There was no city to speak of, only small villages and many farms which really had a hard time producing crops from this extremely rocky part of Italy. The rocks did make it handy for making some sort of foundation and a floor for the tent accommodations. The tents were much like those in North Africa, but at least here the dust seemed to have disappeared. All four officers shared one tent and soon had it looking spick-and-span with plenty of pin up pictures pinned to the tent wall. Rita Hayworth seemed to be the favorite, but Betty Grable was a close second.

The tempo of the activity picked up until it seemed that all were on a speedway. All realized that in less than 10 days this squadron would be flying in actual combat. Each plane had a hard stand assigned to it with a ground crew whose job was to service that plane thoroughly, and an armament crew whose job was to see that the bombs and ammunition were loaded properly.

TRAGEDY

May 31, 1944—PANTANELLA, ITALY

About 2 a.m. on May 31 a jeep drove up to the tent housing the officers of Tipton's crew and the tents of the other pilots who had been alerted for a mission on that day. Likewise, enlisted men throughout the base were being awakened for the mission. Tipton, Burda, Weiss and Krzyzynski all rolled out of their cots. Half asleep they went to the latrine area to shower and return to the tent. After dressing they walked to the mess tent where there was a certain excitement in the air. All of the alerted crews were having a typical army breakfast and all were trying to guess where the mission of the day would take them.

After breakfast the enlisted men were taken to the stand where the planes were parked. On this particular day Tipton's crew was not flying "The Crescent of the Half Moon," but had been assigned another plane. When the enlisted men arrived at the plane the ground crew was just finishing getting the plane ready for the mission. The fuel was topped off and the plane was fully armed with bombs and plenty of bullets for the machine guns. Tipton's crew then went to their individual stations and made sure that everything was in working order. Jasicko, in particular, since he was crew chief, made an inspection of the plane from end to end.

Meanwhile the officers had assembled at the briefing hut where the briefing started at 3 o'clock. On that particular day Henry Willett was the briefing officer. He dramatically removed the sheet from the board revealing the map of Southern Europe which showed a tape running from Pantanella to Ploesti in Rumania. A gasp went up from the assembled officers. They knew that up to that time the bombing of Ploesti was by far the most dangerous mission of any flown.

In the first place it was a long flight, the longest flown up to that time. This meant that if there should be any engine trouble or trouble with the plane's operation it would be very difficult to get back. Also, the flight was, except for that part over the Adriatic Sea and small parts of Yugoslavia, all over enemy territory with enemy fighters a constant threat. On the other hand fighter protection for the squadron would be limited because of the length of the flight. The worst thing of all, however, was the flak. Because the German war machines depended on petroleum products for its day to day operation of tanks, vehicles, planes etc. the oil fields and oil refineries at or near Ploesti were vital to the German war effort. Therefore, there were flak batteries completely surrounding the area which made the Ploesti area the most heavily defended area in that part of Europe.

After a briefing on the flying aspects of the mission the weather officer was called upon to brief the crews on the weather to be expected on the long flight. On this particular day the weather did not look unfavorable for most of the mission, but it was also favorable for the enemy fighters. Then the Intelligence Officer gave a briefing on the enemy positions and fighter strength in different areas. He then ended by describing the mountainous areas of Yugoslavia where Tito's Partisans had control. He explained the procedures to be followed if planes were to ditch in the Adriatic Sea.

Willett then explained some crew changes and told Tipton that Captain Wray from Operations would be flying as his co-pilot on the mission. With that announcement Lt. Weiss had a feeling of relief on the one hand, and a feeling of regret on the other. The crew by that time had a strong bond between all of the crew members and they really did not like strangers inserted with whom they had not had any experience of their capabilities.

After the briefing Lt. Weiss, and some other officers who were left behind, returned to their tents to go back to bed. The rest of the crews were transported to the stands where their planes awaited them. Tipton checked with Jasicko who informed him that everything was O.K. as far as the plane and its armament were concerned. Tipton then told the crew their destination and passed on all of the information given to him at the briefing.

When all was ready and all engines started, a big flare shot up into the sky and the lead plane started down the runway. Thereafter plane after plane took off in short intervals until the whole squadron was airborne. The lead plane would fly in a huge circle so the following planes could close into formation. The planes wanted to fly very close to each other on this mission to give the maximum protection to each with their six sets of machine guns. As soon as the formation was completed, the flight headed east and was soon over the Adriatic Sea. As soon as the Coast of Yugoslavia came into sight all gunners manned their guns and kept a lookout for enemy fighters. However, at that time the squadron still had protective cover from a squadron of P-38 fighter planes and no enemy planes appeared.

The squadron flew at about a 24,000 foot elevation and it was bitter cold. The crew had on their heavy flight jackets and pants and, in addition, the excitement of the flight kept them warm. Soon after the friendly fighters left the formation the enemy fighters appeared. Fortunately, on that day the enemy fighters seemed to concentrate on the 784th Squadron and not on the 785th. The fighters were trying to get in close enough to down the bombers and it seemed that every machine gun in the whole squadron was going off at the same time. Holcomb reported that he saw two enemy fighters go down, and Farrar reported the sighting of a B-24 in trouble. He reported that he counted eight parachutes opening, but that was all.

As the squadron approached the target the enemy fighters pulled back. The reason for this was that the area was now covered with bursts of flak. The flak would come in bursts of four and the huge explosions could rip a plane apart. The sky ahead seemed to be solid flak, but there could be no turning back. It was especially dangerous now that the bombers were on the bomb run. When the bombardiers took control of the plane for the final bomb run the plane had to maintain the same altitude and direction throughout the run until the bombs were released. Lt. Krzyzynski, in effect, took control of the plane during this crucial time. He kept his eyes on the Norden bomb sight with the cross hairs never leaving the target. He inserted the air speed, altitude, wind direction and other information into the bomb sight. At the proper moment the bombs were dropped.

At that time the flak seemed extra heavy and the crew saw one plane have its entire wing torn off. The plane flopped crazily like a wounded bird. Few chutes were seen coming from that plane. One plane was hit while it still had its bombs and with a terrific explosion the whole plane blew up. No survivors were seen. Pieces of the plane ripped into the adjacent plane and it also went down.

Just when it seemed that Tipton's plane would emerge from the flak area there were two huge explosions felt by the entire crew. The crew reacted like the seasoned veterans they were. Jasicko, the crew chief, immediately checked all readings of the engines and saw that the two engines on the right side were malfunctioning. The gunners remained at their posts, more alert than ever. Burda, the navigator, immediately began plotting the most direct flight to semi-friendly territory. Tipton kept busy just trying to keep the plane flying straight and level, an almost impossible task. Capt. Wray, acting as co-pilot, took a visual check of the damage. Soon the intercom system was full of reports. It seemed that the enemy had scored two direct hits, both of them hitting an engine on the right side of the plane. There were numerous other flak holes throughout the plane, but no major other damage at that time. Luckily they had already dropped their load of bombs or else the entire plane could have easily been blown right out of the sky.

The physical strain on Tipton was terrific. With two engines out on the same side of the plane, the other two engines were pulling the plane around. Tipton was trying to fly it on the course which Burda had given him. Also, because of the drag created by this flying method, the plane soon started to lose altitude.

Needless to say, every member of the crew knew what it meant to drop out of formation. The enemy fighters loved it when they could catch a straggler. Then they would all pounce upon the victim like birds of prey. Since the squadron was now out of the flak zone that danger, at least, was not of major concern. The gunners were extra alert. They knew what could be coming.

Though the remainder of the squadron tried to slow their speed and lower their altitude to protect this wounded plane and its fighting crew, they all knew that they could not continue this course of action forever. The first consideration was to get the remaining planes and crews back to Pantanella with as few casualties as possible.

In one of those unusual happenings, which cannot be explained, Eugene Weiss, who had been left behind so that Capt. Wray could fly in his place, was sitting on his cot in the tent of the Crew's officers. At that moment he felt a cold chill throughout his body. The pin-up pictures above the cots of Krzyzynski and Burda fell to the floor. He looked at his watch and realized that the bombs should have been dropped by that time and the planes heading home. However, he could not shake that feeling of dread.

As the plane dropped lower and lower most of the balance of the squadron started to pull ahead of the stricken plane. However, by this time the plane was approaching Yugoslavia and Tipton had ordered all excess material, even guns, to be thrown from the plane. They were getting closer and closer to the ground and ahead were the mountains of Yugoslavia. Two of the planes of the squadron had left the squadron and still stuck close by Tipton's plane to give assistance if they could. Lt. Kennedy, Tipton's closest friend was the pilot of one plane and Lt. Roberts was the pilot of the other. The navigator on Lt. Roberts crew was Don Barrett, Burda's best and closest friend. Tipton's plane kept getting lower and lower and finally was actually flying below the crests of the mountains. When it finally disappeared down a valley, all that the Kennedy and Roberts crews saw was a dark cloud caused by the explosion of the plane. Don Barrett laid his head on the navigator's table and the tears flowed unabated. Every member of those two crews thought they had lost some of their best friends.

Lt. Weiss, meanwhile, had gone to the hard stand where Tipton's plane was to return. The ground crew had already arrived and they were all waiting the return of the squadron. Finally, the first few planes arrived. Those carrying wounded, after shooting flares into the air, were given priority in landing, except for those planes that were totally or partially disabled. Several planes came in on only three engines or with one or more tires shot up and with other parts of planes totally disabled. From the sight of these planes the ground crew and Lt. Weiss could see that this had been and extra hard mission. The last two planes to land were the planes piloted by Lt. Kennedy and Lt. Roberts. When no other planes came into view, Lt. Weiss went to the next stand where the plane of Lt. Roberts had just arrived and spoke to Burda's friend, Lt. Barrett. Lt. Barrett told him that the plane had crashed and that no one in either plane had seen any survivors. He again broke into tears. Lt. Weiss also had tears streaming down his face and the two men silently embraced for a full three minutes.

However, what the Roberts and Kennedy crews did not know was that just as the plane dipped under the last crest, Tipton gave the order to bail out. At that time the plane was only about 600 to 700 feet above the ground. Tipton, by brute strength, seemed to keep the plane up long enough for the entire crew to bail out. Each crew member swears that it could not have been more than 15 seconds between the time that their chutes opened and they hit the ground. Immediately after landing, Burda, and most of the crew members, ripped their chutes off and hid with them in the brush and timber in this mountainous country. The nose gunner, Soteropoulos, was not so lucky. He did not have time to have his chute fully open so when he landed he hit with such force that he injured his legs and back quite severely.

Burda was in hiding for about 10 minutes when the whole hillside seemed to be covered with children and adults as one big hunting party. Burda soon saw the red star on the caps of the men and gave a sigh of relief. He then knew that these were the fighting partisans of Marshall Tito. He emerged from his hiding place and the men, women and children rushed to him. The women especially liked the parachute. Burda had packed and carried with him a small bag holding some minor clothes, escape maps, money and a camera. He immediately had one child take his picture holding his parachute. Later, when he saw another group carrying Soteropoulos, he took another picture of that event. He did not realize it at the time, but after that flight it became almost commonplace for crew members to carry such small bags with them on flights. When Lt. Barret and the Roberts crew were later disabled on a mission and flew back as far as Switzerland, they all had learned from Burda and all had survival gear with them.

The partisans escorted Burda and Soteropoulos to a small village in the hills where the houses were mainly of stone. The people sustained themselves with small patches of oats and barley, fish from the streams, and chickens and sheep. The sheep especially were very important to the villagers as they supplied milk, meat and wool. The women used this wool to knit socks, shirts, pants and items of clothing which seemed to be at least twice as heavy as any the crew had seen elsewhere. The villagers also had fish and wild animals to supplement their diets.

Before the sun had set the entire crew had been collected in this small village and were fed and placed in different homes to sleep.

In the morning a general counsel was held in the village. It might be said that since Yugoslavia was the hiding place of people from the entire region that there were Greeks, Italians, Poles, Czechs, and other nationalities in that village. The crew was told that because of the lack of food and accommodations they would have to walk for several days, through the mountains, to finally arrive at an area where the British had set up a hospital. From there they would eventually get to some small pasture where the OSS could have a small plane fly in during the night and swiftly pick them up and return them to Italy. The villagers did provide small donkeys for some of the crew as well as an armed escort through the mountains. Fighting was a common occurrence in this area at this time.

To allow time for the rescue efforts to become organized and coordinated, and to allow some time for Soteropoulos to recover somewhat from his injuries, it was decided to have the crew stay in the village for two more days. Meanwhile, messengers were sent through the mountains with the report of the safety of Tipton's crew. The message was received in a camp near Berane in Montenego where the British had set up a hospital and a communication center. From there the news was relayed to the headquarters of the 15th Air Force and in turn to 781st Squadron. Lt. Barrett was one of the first to hear the good news at the base. He immediately borrowed a bicycle and travelled as fast as he could to the tent where Lt. Weiss was sorting the personal items of his crew mates. Barrett jumped off of the bike and ran into the tent, hugged Weiss and they both danced around the tent and yelled and screamed so that some of the neighbors wondered just what was going on.

Meanwhile in Dickinson, North Dakota, a message had already been received stating that Lt. Vernon Burda was missing in action. LaDonna, Burda's sister received the message and turned to her younger brother, Robert, and said, "What shall we do about this telegram, Botz, since mother is in Boise visiting with Ted?" (Vernon's older brother, also in the Air Force). They quickly phoned their dad who was at work and read him the telegram. They all agreed to call Ted so that he could tell his mother.

They knew that their mother had been under severe strain. She had four sons in the service. Orville, the oldest, was a bombardier with the 8th Air Force in England and Ted had been a bombardier with the Air Force since Pearl Harbor. He had spent months in the South Pacific where he had flown constantly on missions out of Australia and other areas, being awarded the Silver Star for one heroic action. He was now stationed at Gowan Field near Boise,

Idaho. Bert, the youngest son, was in the infantry and was later engaged in heavy fighting at the Battle of the Bulge and was severely wounded at the first crossing of the Rhine river at Remagen. The whole family realized how much their mother had worried about her four sons so they thought it best to inform Ted of the war department telegram, which they did.

Ted, that evening, took his mother in the car to an isolated spot in Boise and after stopping told her in a quiet manner that Vernon was missing in action. He then told her that it did not mean that he was killed or even wounded, but that he was merely unaccounted for. Sylvia, his mother, leaned on his shoulder and Ted put his arms around her and they both remained silent for several moments while the tears came to the eyes of both of them. After composing themselves somewhat they returned to their house. Mother Burda only hoped that the coming invasion would shorten the war and that her sons could return home to her. She hoped that her other son, Bob, would not have to leave her like this. (Bob, however did serve his country in the Korean War in a later year.)

Dickinson, North Dakota, and the Burda family were just typical examples of the sacrifices made by the Americans at the home front. The country was totally united against a common enemy and all citizens had a common desire to do all they could to help in the war effort. Essentials such as gasoline were rationed and the Burda family had even turned over to the government their large collection of Indian Head pennies and any scrap metal or other items for recycling. Women throughout America answered the call for workers to work in defense plants, and many young women left their home towns, such as Dickinson, and moved to Los Angeles, Portland, or other areas, where they could help directly in the war effort.

Meanwhile, in the small Yugoslavian village Tipton's crew were the guests of honor at a wedding which was celebrated by everyone in the village. After the wedding someone played on a small accordion and the villagers danced and sang and had a gay time and drank many toasts to Marshall Tito, their hero, to the allies helping them in their fight, and to Tipton's crew.

Finally the crew and their escorts started the long journey through the mountains towards Berane. At some spots the trail was only wide enough for the small donkeys to barely get between the wall of the mountain and a drop off of hundreds of feet. The group could only make about 10 miles or less per day but finally approached the British camp. Here they were greeted by the senior British officer who informed them that they had sent the message of their escape to the U.S. Air Force and gave them accommodation until they could be rescued by the OSS. While at that location, Deironimi rushed up to the crew and said, "I have been speaking Italian to some of the Italians in the camp and they just informed me that on this day, June 6, the Allies had invaded France." The whole camp suddenly exploded in expressions of joy. People hugged each other and in five or six different languages expressed their hope that the war was finally on its way to being brought to a close.

The conditions in the camp were hard to describe. It seemed like utter chaos as refugees from many small nations crowded into a small area with little housing and no adequate facilities for the basic needs of these people who refused to give up. Fighters of every nationality were constantly coming and going with guns on their backs and ammunition in their hands. The women should be given special thanks. They did the cooking over small camp fires, hauled water from the mountain streams, took care of the children, acted as nurses, and often joined the men in the fierce fighting with the Germans.

It must be remembered that although German soldiers somewhat controlled the valleys, they could not, and did not, control the hills and mountains. In fact, the German convoys, when driving through territory controlled by the partisans, were only too often completely wiped out. Because of this the average German soldier did not show the bravado that the soldiers who conquered France and other areas showed. They knew that death faced them from many directions, and they did not like it.

The medical facilities were crude, to say the least. Large tents housed the wounded and medical supplies were at a premium. How the British supplied what they did was a miracle. Drugs were extremely short in supply. Some of Tipton's crew actually saw one soldier whose leg was completely shattered merely be given a cigarette instead of pain killing drugs and submit to an operation where his entire leg was cut off, the pain evidently acting as an opiate.

Tipton was finally notified that a small plane would be landing in a small clearing about one day's walk from the camp soon, and that the crew should be getting ready to leave. The crew gathered their belongings together and walked most of the night until they arrived at a small pasture. They were told that the plane carrying supplies and ammunition for the partisans would arrive just before dawn and the time it had on the ground would be extremely limited. This field was only two miles from German troops. The partisans, in the light of the early dawn, lit small fires around the perimeter of the small field and a C-47 suddenly appeared and immediately landed. Supplies and ammunition were unloaded at a break neck speed and wounded partisans were lifted into the plane. Then Tipton's crew crowded aboard. Tipton wondered if the plane could actually make it on takeoff with this overload, but it did.

After takeoff the pilot flew the plane at an extremely low altitude to avoid detection until over the sea. Once over the sea it seemed that the entire body of people relaxed and for the first time became confident that they were really going to escape from the Germans. The plane flew to an allied airfield near Bari where all disembarked. Tipton's crew were transported back to Pantanella where they were greeted as heroes. They were the first crew of the 781st Squadron to get back after being shot down. Eugene Weiss of course was one of the happiest of men to have his crew back. Don Barrett was so happy to see Burda that he borrowed a small motorcycle and with Burda on the back zipped around the camp like a wild man. Unfortunately the bike hit some loose gravel and went out of control. Burda's knee was injured to such an extent and for years the pain would remind him of that episode in his life.

After spending one week at a rest camp on the Island of Capri near Naples, most of the crew returned to active duty. They were informed that they did not have to return to flying status with the 781st but the entire crew, except for Soteropoulos, returned to flying in their original plane, "The Crescent of Half Moon." Paul Brady joined the crew as nose gunner. He told the crew that he felt good about joining Tipton's crew for, as far as he knew, no crew had ever been shot down twice. He did not know that in a little over a month, and after 16 more missions, Tipton's crew was to be shot down again over enemy territory. This time they would not escape.

After D-Day the war effort seemed to accelerate. At least every other day Tipton's crew was flying missions. On July 3 Burda was told that he would be the lead navigator on a flight towards Budapest. The mission seemed to be without trouble and the squadron was flying in formation when the gunners were told to test fire their guns. Suddenly the plexiglass immediately in front of Burda exploded and a missile struck him in the head. Luckily it only cut into his head about 1/4 inch, a half inch more and it would have killed him outright. The bleeding was fierce and because of the blood, Burda could not see. He was taken to the flight deck where first aid was administered. He made it back to the base when the flight returned. After his scalp was sewn up he was given a couple of aspirin, a few more days off, and was awarded the Purple Heart.

On the 14th of July the squadron was on a mission to Porto Marghera with a load of incendiary bombs. Each plane carried twelve five hundred pound incendiary clusters. Since the mission was in Italy, the crews were instructed that if the weather did not permit visual bombing they were to return to the base with the bomb load intact. The fuses would have to be removed before landing. They were time fuses, set to break open the canisters about 5000 feet over the target. This would release the clusters and the fuses were extremely sensitive. When Krzyzynski was trying to defuse the bombs the arming pin came off. The fuse was then alive. Unfortunately the bomb bay doors were malfunctioning. Krzyzynski grabbed the live fuse to his chest, knowing that it could go off at any time. If that happened in the bomb bay, the whole plane, with its crew, would be destroyed. If the fuse had gone off it would have released 110 small incendiary bombs in the bomb bay. Krzyzynski carried that fuse to one of the waist windows and threw the fuse out of the plane. The fuse was barely out of the plane when it went off.

Most of the crew witnessed the incident and thanked God that they had crew members who could be counted on when it mattered. Lt. Weiss wrote the matter up in his diary, which he took on every flight. Weiss did not know, however, that only two days later the crew would be shot down on a flight over Vienna. The information in that diary would not become available until well after the war. It was not until 1992 at a Squadron reunion in Omaha, Nebraska, that Krzyzynski was awarded the Silver Star for his heroic action.

PRISONERS OF WAR

JULY 16, 1944

Tipton's crew was now flying missions almost every other day so, when they were alerted to fly again on the 16th of July, they took it as a matter of routine. The crew had been credited with over 30 missions by now. They had been shot down and survived, had shot down enemy planes attacking their beloved "Crescent of the Half Moon," had been shot at by enemy planes, and hit by flak more often than they could remember. They were a close knit crew and each knew that he could count on his fellow crew members to handle any emergency.

The officers were again assembled in the briefing room before dawn and sat in front of a large cloth covered map. Captain Wray entered the room and dramatically removed the cloth cover. On this day the colored tape showing that day's mission ended at a suburb of Vienna, Austria. This target had been hit before and all knew that the flak was accurate and heavy. The German fighters were expected to be numerous and experienced.

The officers were taken to the hard stand where the rest of the crew had already assembled and performed the usual pre-flight inspections. All engines were started and the planes of the 781st Squadron began taking off shortly after dawn. The assembly went off smoothly and soon all planes were in their fighting formations. Each plane was in a formation giving maximum protective cover to its neighbors on each wing and in front and back. The flight to Vienna was fairly uneventful. The flight pattern was planned to avoid enemy flak as much as possible. The American fighter planes were acting as cover. As the planes approached Vienna the crew could see the field of flak and everyone involuntarily shuddered.

The bomb run started, which meant each plane had to fly a

steady course through the flak. Again the crew saw plane after plane being hit by flak and going down in flames. The crew always tried to count the chutes that ejected. The bomb run was completed successfully and the planes made the turn toward the home base. The entire crew gave a sigh of relief when they finally got out of the flak area. Then the nose gunner, Paul Brady, shouted over the intercom, "Fighters at 12 o'clock high," which was followed by the tail gunner, Farrar, saying, "Another group of fighters at 4 o'clock high." The gunners all manned their guns as the enemy fighters streaked through the sky toward the formation which had already been split by its losses to the enemy flak.

Suddenly, three fighters attacked Tipton's plane and the crew felt the shocks as the plane took hit after hit. Some small fires were started, but soon put out. One engine was directly hit. Tipton told Weiss to feather the damaged engine and increase the power to the other three engines to keep in formation as much as they could. There were leaks in the hydraulic hoses and leaks in the gas lines. Oil from another engine was pouring out. Tipton could not keep up with the squadron. The crippled plane fell behind and slowly dropped in elevation. Smoke billowed from one of the remaining engines, and the vibrations of the plane made it most difficult to fly. The danger of explosion became more certain. Burda again told Tipton the course through Yugoslavia, but before they could reach the mountains Tipton had to order the crew to bail out.

All crew members bailed out successfully and landed in semi-wooded areas near Zagreb. Each crew member quickly covered his chute and hid as much as possible. However, this time they were in territory controlled by the Ustachi who were friendly to the Germans. It was not too long before hundreds of men, soldiers, boys and dogs combed the hills. Before night, all crew members had been captured. They were transported to a small village where they were taken to the small walled city hall and quickly put into small cells in the local jail. The hearts of the crew members sank when they entered the courtyard and saw the huge German swastika flags hanging from the building.

The next day the members of the crew were interrogated. They all refused to give any information except their name, rank and serial number. They were then told that they would be taken to Budapest. There they would be placed in a large stone prison where they would undergo a more thorough interrogation. The next day the crew was taken to the railroad station at Zagreb and put on a train to Budapest.

Upon arriving at Budapest the crew was again put into trucks and transported to the dreaded Budapest prison. The prison was constructed of stone and seemed to be as large as any before seen by any crew member. The members of the crew were herded into one room and the prison guards appeared to take them to their prison room. The guards were small and dressed as if they were in a comic opera. Burda could not help but laugh when two of them stood on each side of Tipton, the largest man in the crew. The guards did not think that was funny. Taking a length of lumber, they beat on Burda until they were satisfied that this course of conduct would not be repeated. The guards did stand in awe of Tipton however. They called him "The Bear." With his huge height and size and with several days beard and matted hair he almost did look like a bear.

The crew was put into a small room with one small window and an extra heavy door, with only mats on the floor on which to sleep. The only toilet facility was a large pot in one corner. During the next few days the crew members were individually interrogated by Germans who spoke excellent English. The crew members still gave only their name, rank, and serial number. The interrogators, however, talked constantly as if they were practicing their English. The crew members were all amazed as to just how much information regarding the crew, the 781st Squadron, the 465th Bomb Group, and other military information the interrogators had.

Every few days the members of the crew could see flights of American bombers flying over Budapest. By evening they could see from their small window a few more American prisoners of war coming into the prison. The crew kept hoping that they might see the Frank Hylla crew in the prison somewhere. That Crew had been shot down over Lake Balaton in Hungary on June 30. It was felt that, if any of them had survived, they might be in the prison in Budapest. After the war was over, Frank Hylla, the pilot, told the members of Tipton's crew, at a reunion of Stalag Luft III survivors, that his plane was on fire when shot down, and only eight crew members got out. Two went down with the burning plane. Frank was taken to a Hungarian military hospital with first, second and third degree burns over his head and hands. His navigator, Jerry Jolicour, was badly burned. Both he and Hylla were transferred to a civilian hospital. Jolicour had gone through navigation school with Burda and was a close friend. Hylla's entry in a wartime log he kept stated that on July 10, "One of the saddest days, Jerry died at 10 p.m. from burns received." On August 8 Frank was allowed to visit the grave of his comrade, and the tears flowed.

It was not until August 9 that Hylla entered the prison at Budapest where he was put into solitary confinement. He was beaten on his bandaged hands and then on his back. On many days, from his small window, he actually saw prisoners being hung in the courtyard by the dreaded SS. The SS were the Nazi's special police, and in most areas were a law unto themselves.

Tipton's crew left Budapest prior to Hylla's coming there. They were put on a train with several hundred other prisoners and went through Vienna and Prague to Stalag Luft III at Sagan, Germany (now Zagan in Poland). When the train went through Vienna the crew saw for the first time hundreds of civilians, beautiful parks, and pretty girls. It made them wish they were home with their loved ones.

When the train pulled into the main train station in Prague there were many Czech women with Red Cross uniforms who had prepared coffee and rolls which they wanted to give to the prisoners. The German guards tried to stop them, but the Czech women refused to be daunted by their threats. In one great mass they pushed their way to the windows of the train. Many of the prisoners remembered this incident for the rest of their lives. Jasicko and Burda, the Czech members of Tipton's crew, were extra proud of the actions of these determined Czech Red Cross women.

Tipton's crew had been told that they would not be permitted to be together after Budapest. In the German prison camps the officers and the enlisted men were separated. Flying officers were given special treatment. The officers of Tipton's crew were taken to Stalag Luft III, in which there were about 10,000 English and American air force officers held in five compounds. The enlisted airmen of Tipton's crew were taken to Stammlager Luft IV near the Baltic Sea, between Danzig and Stettin.

STALAG LUFT III

The prisoner of war camp at Sagan, Germany (Later Zagan in Poland) was to become one of the most famous prison camps because of the daring escapes of numerous prisoners. This was later detailed in the book "The Great Escape," and was made into a movie with the same title.

Sagan was a small city, 80 to 90 miles southeast of Berlin. It was located in the midst of a forest composed of small pine trees. The camp itself was comprised of five compounds designated North, South, East, West and Center Compounds. Center and East Compounds were separated from North, South, and West Compounds by an area larger than the compounds. Here the German personnel were stationed and the administration of the camp was carried out.

Each compound was separated from any other by two parallel barbed wire fences about 10 feet high which were 6 to 8 feet apart. They had vertical and horizontal wires spaced so that prisoners could not squeeze through either fence without cutting the wires. Between the two barbed wire fences were rolls of barbed wire. Guard towers which were approximately 30 feet in height were located about every 100 yards. These towers were manned day and night by German guards with machine guns. Huge spot lights were on each tower and they would sweep the compounds throughout the night. About 10 to 20 feet inside the fence, and completely around the camp, was a single wire called the "trip wire." All prisoners knew that if they crossed over that wire the guards had authority to shoot them immediately. Next to the "trip wire" was a walking or jogging track where the prisoners got their exercise. They also communicated information to each other which they did not want the Germans to hear.

There were from eight to fifteen barracks in each compound.

Each barracks was separated into small areas where several prisoners lived as one family. These were called "Combines." Each combine had from 10 to 12 prisoners with double or triple bunks with a small cooking stove in each area. The bunks were floored with wooden slats on which were placed straw pads. The prisoners operated the combine as a commune, with all work being shared and rules of conduct being obeyed strictly. Lack of fuel and lack of food made living in the barracks unpleasant, but bearable. One must remember that these were well established camps and that some of the prisoners had been captives for several years.

The Red Cross, the Salvation Army, and the YMCA had contacts in the camp and contributed greatly to relieve the suffering of the prisoners. The International Red Cross would send in inspection teams to the camp periodically to see that the Articles of War relating to prisoners of war were not violated. Actually the German Army and the German Air Force strictly complied with these rules as much as they could. The only break down came after the news of the "Great Escape" came to the attention of Adolf Hitler and he ordered all of the escapees to be killed. It was reported that the German High Command objected to this. Hitler changed his orders so that about half of the captured escapees were killed.

To better understand just how the "Great Escape" came about one must first understand the highly secret operations of all compounds and especially the operations of the "X-Committee" members. Except for the constant thought of food, the next most important thoughts of the prisoners was the thought of escape. The camp was comprised of talented men of every trade or profession and these men willingly devoted their talents to the X-Committee. There were printers who could forge passports and legal identification papers of every kind. There were tailors who could take scraps of cloth or blankets and sew garments of every kind including German Army uniforms, civilian clothes of forced laborers from almost any country, suits, and coats of every kind. There were language instructors to teach almost any language used in Europe. There were tinsmiths, metal workers, electricians and many other talents represented by the prisoners. Under the guidance and direction of the X-Committee they all combined their talents whenever needed.

It must be remembered that in the "Great Escape" of March 24, 1944, there first had to be a marvelous piece of engineering and design for the escape tunnels called "Tom, Dick and Harry." The tunnels had to be dug deep enough to avoid detection gear. The tunnel of "Harry" was almost 350 feet long. This required an entrance point which could not be found by Germans, ventilation, a means of carrying the waste sand from the excavation, lighting and an assortment of tools. This operation was doubly difficult as the soil was loose sand of a very light color which could be easily spotted by the Germans.

Tools and ventilation systems were made by craftsmen from kitchen knives and mostly from the tin cans which came with the Red Cross parcels. One item in those parcels was a can of powdered milk with the name "Klim," (milk spelled backwards). These cans were the largest cans in the parcel and the tin was used for almost any conceivable use including "Kriegie Burners," very small heating units on which to heat about two or three cups of water at a time. They were designed like a small forge with a small fan forcing air into another can with a grate of tin. This forced air would enable each prisoner to burn almost anything as fuel including cloth or small bits of wood from the sub-floor, the slats of the beds, or the small twigs in the air raid trenches.

For the great escape, the ventilation system was made up of hundreds of feet of ventilation pipe made from Klim cans, which were secretly donated by everyone in the camp. The bellows to force the air into the pipe were of a design which used wood and other materials. The bellows had to be pumped constantly to get enough fresh air into the tunnel to keep the workers alive.

The sand was a huge problem. Because it was sand, it would cave in on the workers. This happened several times. The biggest problem, however, was the fact that the sand was a totally different color from the soil on the surface. This meant that tons and tons of sand had to be disposed of, without alerting the Germans. Some sand was disbursed by mixing it with the sand in the volley ball courts and some was mixed in the garden area and some in the latrine or toilet area. Most of the sand, however, was disbursed by having the prisoners carry small bags of sand inside their trousers. When they would walk or jog around the track around the perimeter of the camp, they would slowly release the sand which would mix with the loose soil of the track.

The designated escapees had to be fluent in some European language, as well as some German; and they were supplied with all necessary papers and clothing, usually clothing of the forced labor. On the night of March 24, 1944, the escape plans were put into effect. When the first man emerged from the Tunnel the prisoner found, to his horror, that the tunnel was about 30 feet too short. The exit was that far from the pine forest. He waited until the spot light swung past his exit, then ran into the forest. Almost 80 prisoners escaped in this manner before the escape plan was discovered.

Of all of the prisoners that escaped that night, only three made it all the way back to England. Rocky Rockland and Jens Muller made it to a Baltic Sea port where Swedish sailors hid them until the ship landed in Sweden. It took Bob Van Der Stok almost four months to finally escape all the way. He posed as a Dutch worker and took different trains all the way to Holland. He stayed for about six weeks in Holland, until the Dutch underground got him to Belgium where he spent another six weeks. The next leg of his journey took him to Paris and, finally, to the Pyranees mountains, where the French Marquis guided him through the mountains to Spain.

All the rest of the escapees were captured. When news came out that approximately 50 had been shot on Hitler's orders in violation of the International rules, it almost caused a riot. This was a grave concern, even to the German General Staff.

Although the so-called "Great Escape" happened almost five

months before the officers of Tipton's crew entered Stalag Luft III, the story of that planned escape and of the shooting of the 50 escapees, had been told time and again throughout the armed forces of the United States. Tipton retold that story to the others when he found that they were headed to that very camp.

Upon arriving at the camp, Tipton was told that his officers would now be split up. He and Burda were to go to Center Compound, and Weiss and Krzyzynski would go to one of the other compounds. Saying farewell to each other was one of the hardest parts of the whole episode so far. This crew had a special bond which remained with them for the rest of their entire lives. Each man wondered to himself when they would meet again, if ever.

Tipton and Burda were escorted to Center Compound and upon entering they were placed in a position of going through two parallel lines of Kriegies, as the inmates were called. As the men walked slowly through this line, they could hear shouts of joy and laughter as older Kriegies would recognize one or more of the newcomers. In fact, this was a real test to determine whether a new Kriegie would be accepted into this closely knit and highly organized compound. Pity the man who might have been shot down on his first or second mission and was not recognized and vouched for by some older member or members of the compound.

The operations of the escape committees, the communications committees, and the various other internal committees were highly secret and had to be kept from the Germans. The Germans, on the other hand, had an ongoing operation to break up those secret operations. It was known that the Germans would often attempt to infiltrate the camp by having a spy enter as a shot down and captured American. If he was not vouched for by one or more of the fellow Americans, it would be as if he had a highly infectious disease. No one would associate with him more than absolutely necessary. Any secret information would not be mentioned around him.

Tipton and Burda did not have this sort of trouble. All along the line they would hear shouts of "Hey, Tipton," "Hey Burda" and other greetings. They soon met friends from their high school and college days, as well as from their squadron in Italy. They were immediately accepted and entitled to be briefed on all of the operations of the various committees. Of course, some of the secrets were so vital that only a handful of the prisoners, not over 5 or 6, were informed of those matters.

Tipton and Burda were escorted to their barracks, number 43, where they were introduced to the fellow members of their room. The members of each room were jointly called a "combine" and each new member had to be fully informed of rules of that small group. They met fellow officers Schauer, Froeschle, Brockmeier, Keeffe, Lawrence and others. Burda was happy to meet Froeschle who was originally from Hazen, North Dakota, while Burda was from Dickinson, North Dakota. Also, Rudy Froeschle could speak excellent German, which gave him an advantage in getting information from the German guards.

Each member of the combine had to perform his share of the common duties such as cooking, cleaning the combine area, and keeping himself as clean as possible. Some of the prisoners had been prisoners for several years. As a result they had received letters and parcels from their homes and had excess items of clothing or books to share with the others. When one of them would get a letter from home they would share its contents with the others. Tipton and Burda, in their ten months of captivity, never did receive any mail from home and did appreciate the small favor of sharing some of the mail of the other prisoners. When one prisoner would get a letter from his wife or sweetheart that had perfume on it, practically every man in the whole barracks would line up. They would be allowed one sniff of that wonderful letter per man.

The prisoners would try to keep busy during the daylight hours. Those who could would teach classes to other prisoners. Rudy Froeschle taught German, Burda taught Commercial Law, and others taught other courses. This informal school was called "Sagan University" by the prisoners. Other prisoners organized teams for many sports. The equipment was furnished through the courtesy of the Red Cross or Salvation Army. And, of course, all prisoners were encouraged to walk around the perimeter of the compound as much as possible to keep in good physical shape. Escape was always on the minds of the prisoners, being second only to thoughts of food.

Much of each day was spent in your own bunk, especially when the days became shorter and colder. During those times the members of the combine would talk to each other, sharing intimate affairs in their lives with each other. One cold day, in the latter part of December, when the news of the war was not the best because the Battle of the Bulge was being fought, Tipton turned to Burda and said, "Say, Vern, when was the last time you heard from your family, and where are the rest of the famous four Burda brothers, as far as your know?"

"Tip, you know I haven't received as much as a note since we were shot down. But I do think and day-dream about my three brothers, who on the date we were shot down were actively engaged in heavy combat with the enemy. We had a very close relationship as we grew up in North Dakota. We were not far apart in age. In fact, Orville, Ted and I were in high school at the same time—in different classes, of course. Bert was not far behind us. We did everything together."

"I don't know if they are alive, captured, wounded, or dead. Ted was sort of our hero. He was the first to enlist and was flying combat as a bombardier right after Pearl Harbor. He was awarded the Distinguished Flying Cross and the Silver Star. Orville, my oldest brother, finished his training as a bombardier and flew to England. He was fighting with the 8th Air Force at the time we were shot down. Little Bert was the only one of the four who was not in the Air Force. He is in the infantry and was just about ready to go into combat in Europe at the time we were shot down. I have no idea where they are now, but I know they are right in the middle of active combat right now."

Little did Burda realize at the time that his brother Bert, at that moment, was fighting for his life in fierce combat in the Ardennes Forest. He was in the battle which became known as the Battle of the Bulge, where most of his company was captured. Later, his division was the first to cross the Rhine river at the battle at the Remagen bridge. Bert was severely wounded when a fragment from a 105mm shell struck him in the elbow. Much later, in one of the ironies of war, when Vernon was being returned to America on a troop ship as a returning POW, that very ship picked up wounded in England. In the mid-Atlantic, while Burda was standing with his friend and fellow ex-pow, Hal Halstead, he looked down and on a lower deck, to his complete surprise he saw his wounded brother, Bert. This was one of the happiest moments of his life.

Also, unknown to Burda, his brother Orville was now an assistant Group Bombardier in the 389th Bomb Squadron stationed about 100 miles north of London. When the Intelligence Officer of that Group heard that Vernon was a prisoner at Stalag Luft III, he would keep Orville current as to the affairs of that prison camp. When the Russians started to overrun the area, the prisoners were forced to walk in sub-freezing weather, and were later transported to Stalag VII at Moosburg, near Munich, Orville was kept up to date on those developments. One day when Orville and his crew were flying on a bombing mission to Salzburg, his plane flew directly over the prison camp where Vernon was being held. Orville tipped his hat and gave a silent salute to his brother in the camp.

Also, brother Ted had now completed his tour in the Pacific. He was assigned to the 15th Air Force and was now stationed in Italy, near Pantanella where the 781st Squadron was stationed. He went there soon after Vern was shot down and visited with many of the officers and enlisted men who had flown in combat with the Tipton crew and with his brother, Vernon.

None of the Burda brothers could possibly foresee it, but on their mother's 47th birthday—June 20, 1945—all four brothers were reunited at their home in Dickinson, North Dakota. That was surely the happiest and best birthday present any mother, who had just before had her four sons in fierce combat, could possibly have—her four sons survive combat and all four be home safe and sound. Little did Sylvia Burda realize that her fifth son, Robert, would all too soon be involved in combat in the next war—Korea.

Tipton and Burda often thought of Weiss and Krzyzynski and wondered how they were getting along in the West Camp of Stalag Luft III. Many of the prisoners of the West Camp, including Weiss and Krzyzynski, were later imprisoned near Nurnburg until the first part of April, 1945. They were then forced to walk all the way to Moosburg where they entered Stalag VII. Just before being liberated, all of the officers of Tipton's crew were reunited at the prison camp at Moosburg. A happy day it was.

The fate of the enlisted men of Tipton's crew was really unknown to Tipton and Burda. Actually they had been sent to Stammlager IV near the Baltic Sea, about two miles from the small village of Kiefheide, Germany. This camp housed about 10,000 prisoners, mostly enlisted men. The enlisted men of Tipton's crew arrived in this camp after having spent several days cramped in small, dirty boxcars. In an air raid, the prisoners would be left locked in the boxcars, while the Germans hurried to the nearest air raid shelter. Being bombed by one's own air force is an experience that no prisoner will ever forget.

A day's happening in Stalag Luft III and Stammlager IV were about the same. A big part of the prisoner's time was spent in his room. The prisoners had to get up at any time before nine o'clock. There were usually no breakfast rations given by the Germans. Usually in the early morning, everyone had to stand for roll call. At roll call all of the prisoners would be lined up in rows four or five men deep. The German guards would then count to determine if anyone had escaped. When a prisoner had escaped the roll call would really get confusing. The remaining prisoners would shift from row to row or column to column so that the guards could not get an accurate count. After the roll call the prisoners were left to their own devises. Most would just go back to bed. Some played cards, some slept, and some just lay in a type of suspended animation. However, there were many activities in the camp to make the time go a little faster.

Usually about 11:30 in the morning, a type of soup would be brought in which was mostly water, but which sometimes did have some dried vegetables including Kohlrabi, which was like wood. Sometimes there might even be a piece of stringy meat, of uncertain pedigree. They might also serve blood sausage, which most prisoners could not force themselves to eat. The evening meal was usually cooked in the combine with the food from the Red Cross parcels. The American Red Cross parcels contained sugar, oatmeal, spam, powdered milk (Klim), a D-Bar (concentrated chocolate), dried prunes, cigarettes and some other items. The parcel was supposed to be enough for one man for one week, but it had to last for two weeks.

Many of the prisoners who had been in camp for several months had received parcels from home with cookies, candy and items of clothing. All of these items were traded easily in the camp store called "Food Acco." Some say that the name was put on by the early British or Canadian prisoners and stood for "Food Account" but most Americans seemed to think it stood for "Food and Tobacco." At any rate, at the Food Acco a prisoner could trade items he did not use or want for which he would be given points in his account. He then could use these points to buy other items. Cigarettes and the chocolate D-bars were worth the most points. Those who did not smoke usually came out the best.

Services were also performed for points. Elmer Brockmeier in Tipton's combine took in laundry with the help of Schauer and Jones. Also betting often was done on the basis of points.

One of the big events of the entire period was the so-called "Parcel Bash." Dan Downey seemed to be forever eating. A group of his friends began to place bets that he could eat the entire contents of a Red Cross parcel, except for the cigarettes, in one 24 hour period. The betting became fast and furious. Most of the British bet against Downey and most of the Americans, but not all, bet with him. First there was the training period. Fellow prisoners would walk or jog with Downey constantly to get him in good shape. Others would share their food with him so that his stomach could expand to handle the food. It was like one big training camp. One would think that Downey was training for the heavyweight championship of the world.

Finally the big day arrived. Groups of prisoners watched Downey prepare the food with the help of others. They made all kinds of combinations of the food in the parcel—the last of which was chocolate oatmeal cookies. Dan would eat a while, then he would jog or walk with his friends, then rest, and then eat again. This went on all day and finally just before the time limit was to expire, Dan was down to just two oatmeal cookies left. It surely looked as if those betting with him would win. He stuffed one of the remaining cookies in his mouth. However, he just could not get his body to swallow it. He tried and tried. All of his friends felt as if they were trying to swallow those last two cookies for him. But, alas, the time elapsed with those two small cookies still not eaten.

Burda and Tipton both lost on Downey. However, the big loser was Downey's pilot. Years later Dan Downey's wife told Burda that Downey's pilot had placed three $500 bets. When he lost them, he gave checks for that amount to each winner which were written out on pieces of scrap paper. Sometime, within three years after the end of the war, one of these checks was cashed.

As the war progressed, the German allotment of food and fuel decreased, just when the cold winter weather came on. The progress of the war was followed closely by all prisoners. They not only had the information supplied by the Germans, but had access to information supplied by their own communication equipment which had been successfully hidden from the Germans these many years. Maps were brought up to date on a daily basis, and the prisoners would see that after the Battle of the Bulge, the Allied armies would not be stopped. Also, the Russian Army was advancing at a rapid rate from the East. It seemed only a matter of time until the Russian Army would be at Sagan. "Sagan University" had several classes teaching simple Russian with which to greet that army if they liberated Stalag Luft III.

The prisoners could see hundreds of Germans fleeing westward with everything they owned on their backs. Some were pushing carts, a few had horse drawn vehicles, but most just walked. Some were even seen going by on flat cars on the train, all in freezing weather. The prisoners, in their misery, could feel nothing but sorrow for those people who, at this time, were worse off than they.

Rumors continued to flood the camp. Colonel Spivey and General Vanaman tried to keep the prisoners up to date on the true status. General Vanaman was greatly appreciated. He had been a Military Attache in the American Embassy in Berlin and did know some of the top officers in the German Army. The prisoners felt that if anyone could prevent their getting shot, he could. He seemed to think that the Germans would move the prisoners, rather than let the Russians liberate them. This proved to be a fact.

EXODUS

JANUARY, 1945

At about 9 p.m. on January 27, l945, Colonel Spivey and General Vanaman were notified that the entire camp was to march out on foot carrying nothing. They were further told that anyone attempting to escape would be shot. The Germans had about 150 guards ready to carry out that order. The weather at that time was way below freezing and about a foot of snow was on the ground. Yet, the prisoners were ordered to walk on a march, which could easily turn into a death march. Colonel Spivey told the prisoners that they must at least take packs on their backs and be ready to leave in one hour. In one hour the 10,000 men of Stalag Luft III were standing in their respective parade grounds, in snow about a foot deep and in temperatures far below zero. The prisoners stood in this snow for about half an hour when they were finally allowed to go back into the barracks to await the final order to move out. It was not until about 3 a.m. the next morning, January 28, that the men finally marched.

As soon as the men were back in their barracks for this short time, the big flap started. Prisoners rushed about making packs, bashing food, throwing away useless articles and preparing to move. Joe Doherty ran to the kitchen and started making a huge batch of fudge. It really seemed funny at the time. Everyone's bowels moved about three or four times in the first hour. What excitement.

Burda had previously figured that they would be forced to walk and had made overshoes out of a pair of wool socks with Klim tin can soles. He had made heavy mittens by stuffing German toilet paper between layers of cloth, and had put toilet paper between his two blankets to insulate them better. A backpack was made by sewing one stocking as a top of the bag and having another stocking as the bottom of the bag with a belt as the strap between them.

At the last moment, Burda and Schauer decided to make sleds. They took four bedboards and used two as the platform and two on edge as the runners. The tin from Klim cans was used as runners, being attached by barbs from the barbed wire fences.

The prisoners lined up and left Stalag Luft III in long, long columns. The German guards seemed ready to give up. Many threw away much of their equipment and even seemed to beg for cigarettes or other items from our Red Cross parcel. The German soldiers going East toward the Russian front were either old or young children, dressed all in white battle dress.

At two o'clock in the afternoon, after marching about 15 kilometers, the men of Center Compound entered the town of Halbau (later Ilowa in Poland). The weather was so cold that many had frostbitten hands or feet. Thanks to General Vanaman and Colonel Spivey, the 2000 men of Center Compound were able to find shelter in a small church. Its capacity was about 500 persons. It was so crowded that the men had to sleep in shifts, sleeping between each others legs. There was not room enough in the church for all, so some slept in crypts or huddled in doorways. Burda and Tipton slept on the stairway which went to the choir loft. They saw Colonel Spivey and one other massaging the feet of General Vanaman, whose feet were severely frostbitten.

The prisoners of Center Compound had it far better than the men of the other compounds. This probably was due to the fact that General Vanaman was with them. The men of the other compounds had to either sleep bundled together in the snow, or merely walked all night in a slow, barely moving, line. Needless to say, those men had severely frostbitten hands and feet. The feet were specially subject to frostbite as they would get wet from walking in the snow and their shoes would freeze whenever they stopped.

Tipton and Burda tried to keep track of just what was happening to the prisoners in the West Compound. That was where Krzyzynski and Weiss were. They were told that those men really had suffered from the cold, but that they were holding up well.

Tipton and Burda really worried about the status of the enlisted men of Tipton's crew. They knew that they had also been given orders to move out. They also knew that the weather on the Baltic Sea was worse than that at Sagan and that those men would probably have it worse than they. Little did Tipton know that his enlisted men were forced to march, with little food and no camp, for 86 days. At one point Holcomb just gave up and lay by the side of the road to accept death. Jasicko gathered him in his arms and said, "Hulitt, you can't give up. You can't die. Remember, only two weeks ago you found out that you were a father. You now have a son. I'm not going to let you die."

Whereupon Jasicko put Holcomb on his back and, in the snow and cold, carried him for four days. The rest of Tipton's crew tried to help as best they could, but they were almost exhausted themselves. Nearly 50 years later, when Holcomb's son told the story to Burda, tears came to his eyes. He said he could never express his thanks enough to Jasicko to fully show his appreciation.

Those enlisted men walked and walked in one large circle, with no adequate shelter and no adequate food. The toll on their health was extreme and many did not make it. Only after 86 days of that sort of living were they liberated by the British army.

Meanwhile, the men of Stalag Luft III were continuing their march. Their clothing and blankets became soaked with water and with every step they became heavier. Every yard seemed like a mile. The column extended for miles. General Vanaman had given orders not to attempt to escape, but all were so exhausted that they could not even think of that. The guards were almost as miserable as the prisoners. Most had thrown away all excess items. Some of the prisoners felt so sorry for the old men guarding them, that the prisoners even carried the guns for the guards.

Just before Freiweldau there was a long hill. Many were so weak they had trouble making it. From there the men walked through flat farm land and the wind and cold seemed to blow right through them. They finally came to a small village where they were put up in barns, from 400 to 600 in a barn. It was so crowded that they could not sleep at one time, so half would walk around outside while the others slept. The men had to eat the Red Cross food cold and most had loose bowels. Finally, Tipton and Burda were down to eating just margarine, the only thing left.

The General talked the Germans into letting the men stay in the barns for one extra day to dry out shoes and socks and to rest. The socks were dried by putting them next to the men's body while they slept. Shoes, packs and mittens were fixed during this one day stay. Trading was done with German civilians for onions, hot water and brew, in exchange for cigarettes and soap.

January 31 was a hard, long day. The men walked almost 29 kilometers to Muskau. What made it so bad was the fact that the country was again very hilly and the weather was so uncertain. It would snow one minute and then it would rain the next, sometimes mixed with hail. The sleds were still working O.K., although it was tough pulling them up some of the hills.

At Muskau the prisoners were finally quartered in a pottery factory. It was dry and warm and had lights. It was like heaven to those wet, half frozen, exhausted men. Best of all, they received some German black bread. The prisoners were too exhausted to do much more than eat the bread and sleep on the bare, concrete floor.

On February 1, General Vanaman again talked the Germans into letting the men have one more day there. They washed and shaved and slept. Some men from West Compound and Baleria also came into the factory. Their feet were frozen, and in colors of blue, green and yellow. They had walked all the way with no sleeping stops to speak of. One knew Krzyzynski and Weiss and he told Tipton that they were all right, the last time he saw them.

On February 3, the men got up at 4:30 a.m. and prepared to leave. It was raining and the snow was thawing. Burda broke up his sled. He was really loaded down now, but he was determined not to throw anything away, unless he absolutely had to. They walked about 18 kilometers to Braustein where they were bedded down, again in barns. The men bundled three or four together for warmth.

On February 4, the men were again up before dawn and marched 7 kilometers to Spremburg, the biggest town so far. They went into a permanent German army camp with brick buildings. They were put into garages, and best of all, received some hot German soup. Towards evening the prisoners were marched through the town to the railroad marshalling yards where they were told that they would make the rest of the trip by train.

The Germans crowded the men into old French 40 and 8 (Hommes 40, Chaveau 8) boxcars, which must have been built during World War I. There were from 55 to 60 men in each boxcar plus a guard. The men soon arranged themselves as best they could under the extremely crowded conditions. However, as soon as one would go to sleep he would try to stretch out. Burda, who was sleeping on the floor woke up at one time with four men lying in a zig-zag manner so that he could not move.

The train only made 30 or 40 kilometers that night. Tipton heard that they were going to Nurnburg or Moosburg, near Munich. West Compound, including Krzyzynski and Weiss, did go to Nurnburg while the men in Center Compound ended up in Moosburg. Most prisoners did not care where they went, as long as they got there. The Germans gave the men no water and that did not contribute to any comfort. It got so bad that at one stop Dan Downey got a Trinkwasser of steam water from the locomotive, which was shared by those in the boxcar. Most of the men had loose bowels and some were throwing up, which did not help the sanitary conditions of the car. It was filthy enough when the trip started.

The train got to Dresden about midnight on February 5. The prisoners saw many German troops going toward Berlin and the Russian front. One German told the prisoners that he had fought near Moscow and Paris and now he had to fight in Berlin. He would catch any girl nearby and kiss her. He seemed happy and slightly drunk.

In Chemnitz, the train was in the middle of an air raid. The

Germans locked the prisoners in the box cars when the sirens blew and went to air raid shelters. The prisoners thought it would be ironic to survive up to now, then be bombed by friendly bombs. Luckily, no bombs hit the train, and it suddenly took off like a scared rabbit.

The train arrived at the station at Zwickau soon after dawn on the 6th of February. By now, most of the men were really sick with diarrhea and when the train stopped they just could not stand it any more. They all jumped from the train at the same time. The German guards did not know what to do. They would have had to shoot them all or leave them alone. They chose to leave them alone. A new cloak of nice white snow had just fallen at that time, and one can imagine what it looked like when the prisoners were through relieving themselves. The German civilians were really upset. They probably would have shot the prisoners if they had guns, and if the guards were not present.

After leaving Zwickau, the train was close to another bombing raid in the afternoon. This time the prisoners could see the B-17s and B-24s, and they could not help but cheer.

On February 7th, the long train trip finally came to a close when they arrived at the Munich marshalling yard. The railroad yard was really bombed out and some American POWs were helping fix it up. That afternoon, the prisoners were taken to Moosburg, to Stalag VIIA, They were taken to the north lager which had already been entitled the "Snake Pit." The men were put into a shack with nothing for beds, fuel or food. They were all sick by this time and cold and damp. Everyone was covered with fleas and lice. Morale was at its lowest point. The men stayed in the "Snake Pit" for three days. Burda and some of the others slung a blanket up like a hammock so they could finally get some sleep without having three or four bodies over them.

On February 11 the prisoners went through a search, which was a farce. The men at that time had saws, hammers, maps, nails, wrenches and other items. They had carried these items all the way from Sagan, had acquired them at the pottery factory at

Muskau, or had traded for them from the German civilians. None of the items were taken from then. The men were de-loused, taken to the East Lager, and placed in barracks.

The men were put in tiers of 12 men, 3 bunks high with 6 bedboards per bed. The beds had mattresses of straw and were full of lice, fleas and bedbugs. The prisoners' life in Moosburg started. What a miserable life it was. The weather was cold and damp and the Germans would not supply any fuel for heat. The men would stay in bed all day, except for necessary body functions. There were no facilities to do anything, even if they did get up. The lighting was so poor that some never did see what their bunks looked like. They were so crowded that the only way they had of keeping personal items was by hanging them from the ceiling. Burda had a top bunk and after hanging up his belongings he barely had room to lie horizontally. Sitting up in any of the bunks was out of the question.

The German food ration consisted of one-half cup of warm water for breakfast, one cup of thin, watery soup for dinner, and a little black bread for supper. Now and then they would give a small extra issue of cheese, margarine or blood sausage. There were no Red Cross parcels for some time. Finally the Red Cross did come through with one parcel per man, which was expected to last two weeks. The first parcels were British parcels, which contained food that had to be cooked. The Germans, however, would not provide any fuel. The prisoners then made their own burners, called Kriegie Burners, from tin cans, using barbs from the wire as nails. Burda actually kept his burner and brought it back to show his family.

These burners were a master of engineering. They had a large burning barrel about 6 inches in diameter, plus a small connecting tin rectangle which connected to a small fan about 3 inches in diameter, made from a tin can. The fan blades were also made of tin. On the side was a large wooden wheel, 12 to 14 inches in diameter. This large turning wheel, when cranked, would turn the small fan, which in turn would force air through the connecting tin to the burning chamber. It acted just like a forge in a blacksmith's shop. In this burner almost anything would burn. Almost every Kriegie had one of these burners, or at least there was one burner for every three or four prisoners.

For fuel, the prisoners first burned the bedboards and slung the sacks by nailing the burlap sacks to the sideboards of the bed. When the bedboards were all used up, a little more sabotage was performed—the sub-floors of the barracks were torn out and burned. Also, sticks from air raid slit trenches were robbed and used for fuel. It is reported, on good authority, that when General Patton visited the camp a day or two after liberation, he came stomping through a barrack and his foot went right through the floor. There was no sub-floor under the rotted top floor. He really blew up, until the matter of the missing sub-floor was explained to him.

The latrines were to handle the waste affairs of 2000 men. The Germans refused to clean them out. What a mess it was. Human waste flooded all over the floor of the latrine and even into the yard. Since everyone was still sick with diarrhea, it really became a mess beyond description. The men were practically wading in human excrement.

The prisoners decided that they absolutely would not cooperate with the Germans for appel (the daily counting sessions) unless this matter was cleaned up, even if some of them would be shot. There were several hours of tension before the Germans finally gave in and promised to clean the latrines.

The fleas, lice and bedbugs were really bad by now. It was not unusual to find one hundred or more bedbugs, fleas and lice in one bed. The prisoners had only the clothes on their back and no facilities for laundry. Because of the cold and lack of heat, all slept in their clothes. Tipton and Burda, and most of the others, had not had their clothes off for over six weeks. They had not washed for just as long either, and this did not help matters.

Hal Halstead solved the problem, somewhat. The cigarette smokers would keep a "Butt-can" near their bunk. They would put the cigarette butts in the can and in turn would combine several butts and make new cigarettes from the first butts. The second butts were made into third butt cigarettes, and on through the fourth butt cigarettes. By the time of the smoking of the fourth butt cigarettes, the smoke would almost kill the men, let alone kill fleas, etc. Hal would take these third or fourth butt cigarettes, pull the blanket over his head, and smoke that deadly item. Needless to say, the fleas, bedbugs and lice made a hurried retreat from his bed. The men often wondered how Hal stood it himself.

Duane Gould became so infected with flea bites that he had blood poisoning. Several fellows had their whole bodies covered with bites. The bites were bad enough, but they itched so badly that you could hardly keep from scratching. As soon as the bites were opened, infection readily set it.

Tipton and Burda were not bothered too much. They could feel the little devils running over their bodies, but they were rarely bitten. As Tipton said, "It was probably because we were so filthy or we may have had the wrong blood type."

Finally, spring came, and the renewed offensive of the Allies started pushing the Germans back. The American and British forces were advancing on Nurnburg so the Germans evacuated the prisoner of war camp there. The prisoners left Nurnburg on April 4, and walked for 17 days to Moosburg. This time, the men had to contend with rain, instead of snow and cold. Krzyzynski and Weiss knew they were going to Moosburg, where they hoped to be reunited with Tipton and Burda. The men looked like drowned rats when they finally arrived at Moosburg on April 21. The first thing that Krzyzynski and Weiss did upon arrival was try to find Tipton and Burda. They were successful and the officers of Tipton's crew were reunited after nine long months of being separated. They each had a wonderful feeling, knowing that each was alive, and that they were together again.

One day, in the latter part of April, the prisoners saw fighter planes scouting the camp. On April 29th the prisoners were ordered inside the barracks. They could hear the sound of big guns, machine guns and rifles. By peering through cracks in the wall they could see Allied infantrymen advancing through the fields and pushing towards Moosburg.

Almost immediately thereafter they heard the sweetest sound they had ever heard—the rumble of American tanks. When those tanks rolled into the prison compound they looked as big as battleships. The Kriegies spilled out of the barracks, unmindful of the live bullets still whistling through the air. They cheered the troops and gobbled the K-rations which the American soldiers of Patton's army threw to them. Those K-rations may not have meant much to the liberating army, but they were like candy to the prisoners.

Then, suddenly and for no apparent reason, a hush fell over the entire camp. All eyes turned toward the center of town, in which stood two high church steeples from the churches on the hill above the camp. Over 20,000 eyes saw machine gun bullets splatter against the steeples. A period of quiet fell, and then it happened—a scene which brought tears streaming down the face of every American prisoner-of-war there, and a sob from every throat. The prisoners saw the greatest sight, and witnessed the most emotional minute they would probably ever witness.

There, raised before their eyes and flying defiantly above one of the church steeples was the symbol of their beloved land—THE AMERICAN FLAG!

As one great mass, all felt emotion, emotion that one who has not been deprived of freedom, one who has not suffered behind barbed wire for months without adequate food, clothes, heat or word of loved ones and of home, could not possibly feel. Yes, the tears flowed from over ten thousand faces that day. Over ten thousand unashamed faces cried as that American Flag shocked them back to memories of that which they held most dear—THEIR BELOVED LAND, THEIR LOVED ONES, THEIR HOME.

Praise for *Desert Oracle*

"Ken Layne's writing shows us that human nature is its own wild thing, sprung from the same source as forests and deserts and oceans, and every bit as unruly . . . In the cities, surrounded by other humans and our constructs, it's too easy to forget that there's anything else . . . but spend long enough attending to the desert or the forest, and you wake up to the whole living world of which you're only a small part . . . *Desert Oracle* is more than a collection of Wild West miscellany for the Instagram crowd, or a catalog of unruly humans in an unruly landscape. It's a lesson in training the heart and mind to attend and honor and listen, over the course of a lifetime . . . Its strength is in the author's plain enchantment with the place that chose him. This isn't just a romantic idea: it's salvation."
—Ellie Robins, *Los Angeles Review of Books*

"The desert is a powerful cocktail of breathtaking beauty, brutality, and mystery. Layne serves it straight-up . . . Reading this book is like swapping tales around the campfire under a star-filled sky." —Michelle Ross, *Booklist*

"After this historic year, perhaps more people than ever are seeking purpose, or simply an escape, and the desert has a little something for everyone. If you want to have an experience with a UFO, a ghost, or God, the Mojave is a good place to go, and *Desert Oracle* can be your guide."
—Jera Brown, *Outside*

"*Desert Oracle* isn't about the sandy suburbia that keeps creeping east, littering the vast plains with chain restaurants and fifty-five-plus communities. It's about the lonely, parched, mythical desert . . . Layne seems to relish telling sly, campfire-like stories."

—David Allen, *The Sun* (San Bernadino)

"[Layne's] essays are a result of a lifetime of love for desert landscapes, lore, and wildlife. There's no patronizing talk about protecting wild areas. Instead, there's a narrative that blends history, science, and the unexplained . . . For all the stories of UFOs and sasquatch-like creatures (called the Yucca Man in the Mojave), the most bizarre, fantastical, and intriguing remain the stories with flesh-and-blood people at the center."

—Jan Pytalski, *The Daily Yonder*

"*Desert Oracle* may seem to target mystics and desert rats, cryptozoologists and RV homesteaders, but it's actually for anyone who has ever been moved by the desert—that strange landscape stripped down to the harshest of elements: sun, rock and sand . . . Flip to any page and you'll find something that could belong in Ripley's Believe It or Not."

—Connor Goodwin, *Inside Hook*

"With his succinct, descriptive, narrative-driven prose, Layne creates a fascinating homage to the beauty of an often unforgiving landscape."

—*Publishers Weekly*